The Teen Guide
to Global Action

How to Connect with Others (Near & Far)
to Create Social Change

Barbara A. Lewis

free spirit
PUBLiSHiNG®

Helping kids
help themselves®
since 1983

Library of Congress Cataloging-in-Publication Data
Lewis, Barbara A., 1943–
The teen guide to global action : how to connect with others (near and far) to create social change / Barbara A. Lewis.
     p. cm.
  Includes index.
  ISBN-13: 978-1-57542-266-4
  ISBN-10: 1-57542-266-2
  1. Social action—Handbooks, manuals, etc. 2. Social action—International cooperation—Handbooks, manuals, etc. 3. Young volunteers. 4. Teenage volunteers in social service. 5. Teenagers—Political activity. I. Title.
    HN65.L4424 2007
    303.48'4—dc22
                                   2007027518

The profiles in this book include information from interviews with youth as well as media reports, Web sites, books, and other secondary sources. Every effort has been made to verify the accuracy of the book's content.

Edited by Douglas J. Fehlen
Cover and interior design by Michelle Lee
Interior illustrations by Chuck U, www.chucku.com, except on pages 29, 87, 103, and 121.
Cover images © istockphoto.com

10 9 8 7 6 5 4 3 2
Printed in the United States of America

Free Spirit Publishing Inc.
217 Fifth Avenue North, Suite 200
Minneapolis, MN 55401-1299
(612) 338-2068
help4kids@freespirit.com
www.freespirit.com

Printed on recycled paper
including 30%
post-consumer waste

Dedication & Acknowledgments

This book is dedicated to courageous teens everywhere. Believe in your talents and abilities. Although you should not feel responsible for tackling world problems, you also shouldn't feel excluded from participating in the process of finding solutions. Many adults today have greater respect for your voice and your ability to think. The growing confidence in the youth movement empowers you to both serve and to be an activist for positive social change. As adults look on and see the gathering strength of the global youth movement, at the idealism, sincerity, and enthusiasm of teens, they must surely support this power or miss Earth's flight into the future.

This book is also dedicated to:

Benjamin Quinto, a courageous youth founder of the Global Youth Action Network, a leader with vision, who won't accept "no" for an answer, when working for youth voice, positive involvement, and rights. He provided generous sharing of information and teen stories. Ben took the time to communicate with me during the many edits of this book, and his patient assistance helped to make it possible. He typifies positive youth action.

All of the young people featured in the book who have struggled to make our world a better and safer place.

Our present and future grandchildren: Jordan, Andrew, Adam, Maddy, Chloe, Anderson, Lizzie, and Ruby. They have already succeeded in making *my* world a better place.

And also to Skyler, Alexa, and Tiana.

I also give special thanks to the following people:

- Judy Galbraith, who exemplifies both integrity and compassion, and who also manages to maintain a good sense of humor.

- Douglas Fehlen, for his advice, constant help, good ideas, patience, and understanding.

- The many organizations who have shared a story for this book. I especially want to express gratitude to: TakingITGlobal, Rotary International, Silvia Golombek and Youth Service America, Plan International of India, the Future Problem Solving Program, OXFAM International, Voices of Youth (UNICEF), the Special Olympics, and Free the Children.

Contents

Introduction

> *Realizing that we have the power to make a positive change and going out and taking action, wherever it may be . . . that's the most important thing.*
> —Mihiri Tillakaratne, 18, Global Activist

Have you ever heard about some problem or injustice and thought, "I wish there were something I could do about that"? Well, most likely there is. Caring and committed young people are working around the world for a better future—and you can, too.

In fact, teens are some of the most active participants in service and social action. In the United States alone, over 15 million young people volunteer with community organizations each year. This doesn't include people working on their own to help others and effect social change.

And it's not just in the United States where teens are involved in helping others. There's a whole movement of youth making a difference all over the globe.

What's Happening Around the World?

How exactly are young people getting involved? Zach Hunter, a seventh grader from Ashburn, Virginia, started Loose Change to Loosen Chains, an organization dedicated to ending modern-day slavery. After seeing how few girls in her Afghanistan village were allowed to attend school, Zuhra Bahman started an organization that gives females more education opportunities. Ilona Seure, upon returning from a service project in Vijayawade, India, became focused on helping youth who are homeless in her native Amsterdam, capital of the Netherlands.

What do all of these teens have in common? They all reached out—across a country or across the globe—to help make the world a better place. Connecting and working with other youth, they're making their dreams of a better future come true.

Zach, Zuhra, and Ilona are by no means alone. More and more teens are getting involved in their own communities and in places far from home. Some even oversee large organizations that have thousands of supporters in many countries. If this sounds intimidating, realize that most

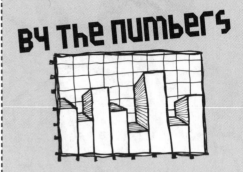

By The Numbers

Youth Involvement:

Just how many teens are involved in service and social action? It's hard to come up with an exact number, but millions of young people turn out each year to participate in Global Youth Service Day. In 2006, for example, the Iraqi Democratic Coalition for Youth Empowerment brought together dozens of students on environmental and beautification projects at three Baghdad schools. In Gardena, California, Habitat for Humanity united Muslims, Jews, Christians, and people of other faiths in building low-cost housing for people in need.

These are only two of countless global projects sponsored by Youth Service America, Global Youth Action Network, and a coalition of world partners. Over the years, Global Youth Service Day has involved more than 30 million young people from virtually every nation. The event takes place annually in April. You can learn how to participate by visiting www.gysd.net.

of these efforts started small—one visit to a shelter, research on the world's refugee crisis, a demonstration in support of preserving rain forests.

DIFFERENCE MAKER

Jyotirmayee Mohapatra

How important is fighting for the rights of women and children? Very important, according to Jyotirmayee Mohapatra of Kendrapara, India. As a teen, Jyotirmayee became fed up with being treated as a second-class citizen and decided to do something about it. She began to work with Nature's Club, an organization focused on improving the lives of girls and women through education.

It turns out Jyotirmayee's work with Nature's Club was just a stepping-stone for bigger things. She decided she wanted to form her own organization, one with a wider focus. And that's what Jyotirmayee did. Meena Clubs are village-based groups working to improve the rights of women and children. The clubs also address challenges facing all of a village's people. Big issues for the groups include equality, education opportunities, improved living conditions, and other important rights.

What started as the passion of one girl has grown into the commitment of many. Thousands of people volunteer at Meena Clubs in Jyotirmayee's district, and there are more than 300 clubs across India. For Jyotirmayee, her action isn't a choice, but a duty—a duty to fight for justice for all people.

The fact is you can take any action of your choosing and on any scale—big or small, alone or with a group. To use this book, it's not necessary to start your own organization or fly to another corner of the globe to make a difference—though both of these things can be really great. You'll find many small, but important, actions you can take to improve your community. And your project may just take on a life of its own.

Why More Youth Today Are Involved in Service and Social Action

Young people today more than ever are seeking opportunities to create a better future. There are a number of reasons for this. One is that as nations become more developed, people often gain more individual rights. There is more awareness of injustices, and more people are working to correct them. Another big factor is the emergence of media outlets—including television, the Internet, and other new technologies. It's now possible to learn about situations all over the world by simply turning on the TV or clicking on a Web site.

The Internet also provides new opportunities to help others without leaving your chair. You can advocate online by spreading the word about a cause and connecting with others to come up with solutions. Social-networking sites give you the opportunity to communicate in new ways—by sharing video, building coalitions, and even holding global meetings via Web conferencing. There are countless other activist applications of the Internet, with many more likely on the horizon.

How to Use This Book

While there are many people working for social causes, much injustice remains in the world—which is where you (and this book) come in. *The Teen Guide to Global Action* can help you make nearly any difference you set your mind to based on your interests and time commitment. Here's what's in this book:

4 Steps to Global Action: This section provides you with background information on service and social-action opportunities. You'll find ideas for deciding which opportunities are best for you, as well as tips on doing research and planning projects.

Connecting with Others: Here you'll discover helpful suggestions for finding and joining groups of teens—those who have similar service goals. There are also steps you can take to create your own organization.

Issues: The rest of the book outlines seven areas in which you can make an impact: Human Rights, Hunger and Homelessness, Health and Safety, Education, Environment and Conservation, Youth Representation, and Peace and Friendship. For each of the issues there are service ideas for smaller home, school, or neighborhood actions ("Keep It Local") and big world contributions ("Take It Global").

Throughout you'll find a number of different features:

QUICK TIPS
What's in It for You?

The best thing about service and social action is the positive difference you can make. But you may also benefit. You have the opportunity to:

➤ make friends (maybe even for life)
➤ learn about other people and cultures
➤ build new talents and skills
➤ appreciate life in new ways
➤ build confidence and leadership abilities
➤ gain recognition for your service
➤ have a lot of fun

Difference Maker: True stories of today's teens making a difference in the world. These inspiring reads can give you many ideas for taking your own action.

Activist Flashback: Stories of teens from the past who have made a big impact on today's world.

Point & Click: Web resources for finding more information on causes, organizations, and helpful tools.

Connect: Youth organizations you can contact to get involved.

Quick Tips: Lists, tips, and other information for making your efforts effective.

By the Numbers: Statistics and other information on issues people face.

Activities: Quizzes and Action Plans to help you decide on and map out your action.

Make Your Difference

We live in an amazing world. It's an awe-inspiring planet full of diverse people, a place that provides for us all. It's also a place that needs to be watched over, its people and resources protected. Whether it's preserving the environment, promoting public safety, or ensuring equal opportunity, I encourage you to find your place to contribute.

Many young people have come before you. I hope that you are inspired by their stories in this book. Countless opportunities to make an impact remain. I hope you will take advantage of those presented—or come up with your own. Regardless of the contribution you choose to make, I'd welcome hearing from you. I may even be able to include your story or organization in a future edition of this book. You may email your stories to help4kids@freespirit.com or mail them in care of my publisher.

Free Spirit Publishing
217 Fifth Avenue North, Suite 200
Minneapolis, MN 55401-1299

Best wishes to you,
Barbara A. Lewis

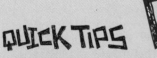

QUICK TIPS

Where Is Action Needed?

Some people believe that only certain areas of the world are in need of development and social movements. The truth is, each nation and region has challenges—large and small—that it must face. No matter who we are or where we live, we can make things better.

4 Steps to Global Action

> *Young people do care; it's just a matter of providing opportunity to get involved.*
> —Annalise Blum, 18, Global Activist

1. Find Your Cause

The first step toward getting active in service or social action is to figure out where you want to make your mark. You might start by thinking about what issues are important to you. Also consider your interests and where they might lead you.

For example, if you really love wildlife, you might enjoy working on a campaign to save a certain species or a habitat that is home to many animals. You might volunteer at a nature center or test for pollution in local lakes or rivers. The opportunities truly are limitless.

What's Your Issue?

If you're not sure where you want to make a difference, try taking this quiz. On a blank sheet of paper, give each activity that follows a number based on how much it interests you.

Scoring Key

1 = No thanks.

2 = Maybe—could be cool.

3 = I'm into it.

4 = Sign me up now!

- [ ] **A.** researching human rights violations
- [ ] **B.** organizing a food drive
- [ ] **C.** petitioning for a traffic light at a dangerous intersection
- [ ] **D.** raising money for schools
- [ ] **E.** conducting a neighborhood campaign against animal cruelty
- [ ] **F.** serving in school government
- [ ] **G.** protesting against war
- [ ] **H.** marching for equal opportunity
- [ ] **I.** starting a public awareness campaign on poverty
- [ ] **J.** organizing a fund drive for the prevention of cancer
- [ ] **K.** writing profiles of young people who have no access to schooling
- [ ] **L.** informing people about global warming
- [ ] **M.** serving as a student ambassador in another country
- [ ] **N.** volunteering to build infrastructure in a war-torn country
- [ ] **O.** lobbying organizations for equal compensation regardless of race or gender
- [ ] **P.** working in a shelter for people who are homeless
- [ ] **Q.** organizing an anti-drunk-driving campaign
- [ ] **R.** tutoring children in reading or math
- [ ] **S.** organizing the cleanup of a local park
- [ ] **T.** setting up a youth chapter of your local government
- [ ] **U.** creating a Web site that outlines your views on conflicts

Scoring

When you are finished with the quiz, use this scoring key to find your preferred topics. On your sheet of paper, add up the numbers for the follow groups of letters:

Group 1: A + H + O = ____ (Human Rights, pages 31–44)
Group 2: B + I + P = ____ (Hunger and Homelessness, pages 45–56)
Group 3: C + J + Q = ____ (Health and Safety, pages 57–70)
Group 4: D + K + R = ____ (Education, pages 71–82)
Group 5: E + L + S = ____ (Environment and Conservation, pages 83–97)
Group 6: F + M + T = ____ (Youth Representation, pages 98–111)
Group 7: G + N + U = ____ (Peace and Friendship, pages 112–125)

The point totals among the groups can give you an indication of your deepest interests and concerns. For example, if you have 12 points for a group, it's pretty likely that a project involving that topic would be a fit for you.

QUICK TIPS

Sources of Inspiration

Where do people get their ideas for service?

➤ hobbies, talents, or subjects at school
➤ concerns about global or community challenges
➤ interests of friends or family
➤ news items on TV or the Internet
➤ information from meetings, assemblies, or faith services
➤ articles in newspapers or magazines

Iqbal Masih and Craig Kielburger

The 1995 newspaper headline read, "Battled Child Labor, Boy 12, Murdered." Craig Kielburger, from Toronto, Ontario, was shocked when he read the article. He was the same age as Iqbal Masih, the Pakistani youth who had been shot dead while riding his bicycle. Iqbal's story was a very sad one. At age four, he was sold into bonded labor—a form of slavery. Chained, beaten, and poorly fed, Iqbal was forced to work in a carpet factory for 12 hours a day, six days a week. All he really wanted to do was go to school, but it seemed Iqbal would grow old in that factory.

But life held more in store for Iqbal. At the age of 10, he escaped his captors. By 12, with the aid of a human-rights organization, he began speaking out and leading children against child labor—not only in Pakistan, but also in countries far from home. People from many nations began to stop buying the carpets produced by slave labor. Unfortunately, this angered many in Pakistan—especially the powerful factory owners who were losing money. Some people believe those factory owners were responsible for Iqbal's murder, but no one knows for sure.

Fast-forward ahead to Craig Kielburger's reading about Iqbal's death in the newspaper. Craig didn't know what child labor was. It did not take him long, however, to find out. It also did not take him long to begin sending letters, giving speeches, passing petitions, and fundraising on behalf of enslaved youth. A visit to south Asia helped Craig better understand some of the harsh realities many young people face. The trip also strengthened his resolve to make a difference in their lives.

With the support of family and friends, Craig founded Free the Children—an organization based in Toronto and dedicated to ending the mistreatment and exploitation of youth around the world. Over 10 years later, the organization is no longer made up only of Craig's family and friends, but over 100,000 youth. Programs have supplied education materials, medical supplies, sanitation systems, and other necessities to over one million people in nearly 50 countries.

All of this came from the imagination of one 12-year-old boy, Craig Kielburger, whose actions have in turn inspired countless other youth to take up the cause. One young girl released from bonded labor described it best: "The day Iqbal died, a thousand more Iqbals were born."

Connect

Free the Children
www.freethechildren.org
Iqbal Masih's spirit lives on in the work of Craig Kielburger and this organization. Log on to the Web site to learn how you can get involved in one of the many programs geared toward educating and empowering youth.

2. Research Your Cause

You may already know a lot about an issue and have many ideas for potential projects. Maybe you don't. Regardless, putting time into research is very important. The more creative and tenacious you are, the better. To get others' support, you'll need to know your topic well.

Sources of Information

Magazines, newspapers, media reports, and books. These are options for learning more about current events—just remember how Craig Kielburger read about the story of Iqbal Masih. The best approach for lining up research materials can be to visit a library with a database that compiles document records. You can usually search these directories by subject, keyword, and many other criteria. Most larger libraries have their collections online so that you can search for resources from home, if you have Internet access, and request materials be transferred to a location near you.

Internet. There are many Web sites that compile media reports and allow you to sort through items at a rapid rate. Any search engine will also, with a few keystrokes, direct you to organizations and advocacy groups that collect information on just about any issue you might think of. You also can find films, interactive tools, and tons of other practical applications. For detailed Web research suggestions, visit www.internettutorials.net—a site devoted to explaining how the Internet works and effective ways to search it.

Other people. The Internet and print resources are great for many purposes, but sometimes it can also be helpful to talk with and learn from others. Think of experts in the community who might be able to give you information. Connect with people in a mosque, synagogue, church, or another house of worship. Talk with family members, teachers,

QUICK TIPS

Research Pitfalls

When doing research, remember to collect information from a variety of sources that represent different sides of an issue. Web sites, print resources, and other people often are biased on issues and present only information meant to get you to think in a certain way. Newspaper editorials, for example, may take positions on issues to remain aligned with a certain political party. Many personal blogs are short on facts but full of strong opinions. Reference a number of different resources to make sure you're getting the full story on an issue.

local leaders, business owners, and others who understand regional concerns. For those people in faraway places, you might conduct interviews by email, instant messaging, or online chats.

Questions to Ask

The questions you ask are often just as important as the sources you use in your research. What investigative approach will help you be effective with your action? Following are questions to consider as you track down information. It's important to write or type notes on what you find. The information will prove helpful when you're planning your action.

1. What is the situation you'd like to do something about?

2. Where is the problem occurring?

3. Who is affected?

4. Why is the situation happening?

5. Why does something need to be done?

6. What are the short- and long-term effects of the problem?

7. What do people in the affected community want to make happen?

8. What is already being done to address the problem?

9. What groups are involved in the effort to make a change?

10. What can you do?

3. Plan Your Action

Now that you've researched your cause, what action can you take to make things better? Each cause can call for a variety of responses. For example, many people are concerned about world hunger. How they address the problem, however, can vary widely—from organizing local food drives to fundraising for international groups that provide aid.

Following are just a few types of action you might take for a cause. Many other suggestions appear throughout this book.

Volunteer

Volunteer work is one of the most common forms of service. You've perhaps already pitched in at some point to help in a community effort—say to clean up a park or help others in the wake of a natural disaster. Volunteering can take many forms. A pretty simple way to think about it, though, is giving your time to a cause without being paid or otherwise rewarded.

Much of the time, people volunteer with agencies or faith communities in their area to address local challenges. But there are also many opportunities to volunteer (online or in person) with national or international organizations.

Here are a few of the many ways you might give your time:

- Help on an agriculture project promoting sustainable living.

- Tutor children or adults in a school, library, or community center.

- Visit with senior citizens at a retirement center.

- Serve meals to people in need.

- Give your time to an after-school program.

- Work on a housing project for people without homes.

Five Quick Volunteer Tips

1. Be realistic about how much time and energy you will be able to devote to an organization. A good rule to keep in mind is to start with a small commitment and build from there.

2. Volunteer with others. Working for a good cause with family members, classmates, and friends can make your experience even more fun and rewarding.

3. Consider your personal goals when choosing an opportunity. Volunteer work is a great way to build new skills you can use in the future. Choose an activity you know will challenge you.

4. Reflect on your talents and try to match them with the right opportunity. For example, if you're a whiz on the Internet, think about doing Web design or research for an organization.

5. Have a passion for your cause. If you really like teaching others, you might help at a school or literacy center. If animals are more your kind of thing, a local shelter might be a better fit. Here's the bottom line: When you love doing something it's much easier to stay committed to it.

Organize Service Efforts

To make the difference they do, community agencies, national nonprofits, and international NGOs (non-governmental organizations) need staffing, supplies, and funding for other operating expenses. This includes the efforts of many volunteers working behind the scenes to raise money, collect resources, and organize others.

Some ways to organize service efforts include:

- answering the phone at a health center
- finding a business or an organization to sponsor a cause
- taking pledges for donations at a phone bank
- walking, running, or riding a bicycle in a fundraiser for an important cause
- applying for grants or selling goods to help fund a local agency
- performing data entry for an organization

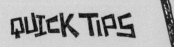

QUICK TIPS

Five Quick Tips for Organizing Service Efforts

1. Set goals. Whether you're raising funds, rounding up supplies, or recruiting people for a cause, set targets for what you would like to accomplish.

2. Advertise and seek media attention. One of the best ways to ensure the success of a campaign is to make lots of people aware of it. Provide some form of entertainment to draw crowds to recruiting or fundraising events. Don't forget to also involve people you know. Ask family members, neighbors, friends, and people from a church, temple, mosque, or another house of worship to join you.

3. When fundraising, make accommodations for handling cash. Know the procedures for collecting and storing money. It's a good idea, for example, to wear a badge or carry another form of identification from an organization to assure potential donors of your credibility. Be prepared to give donors a receipt for their contributions. Also have steps in place for safeguarding funds you collect.

4. If you collect clothing, food, or other items for people in need, make sure you have an adequate location to store goods. This place should be safe and secure from theft. Obtain permission to use the space—whether it's at school, in a community center, or within another neighborhood building.

5. Think about who will be your best volunteers and donors. Capitalize on the support of individuals and civic organizations likely to back your cause. You might contact a local agency to call for volunteers. When fundraising, ask donors whether an employer might match donations.

Advocate for a Cause

Advocacy can include many different actions and be applied to almost any cause. Briefly, it means to work on behalf of a person, group, place, or campaign. Regardless of the issue, advocacy is often a crucial tool for effecting change because it can influence large numbers of people and help create improvement on a wide scale.

Here are a few ways you might advocate for a cause:

- Create a public service announcement (PSA) on a community issue.

- Circulate a petition about a local environmental concern.

- Testify before lawmakers about a piece of legislation.

- Write a letter to the editor in support of a cause.

- Join a public demonstration in support of open and free elections.

- Deliver a speech before a local organization.

QUICK TIPS

Five Quick Advocacy Tips

1. Use the Internet. You might post your views on a Web site. Or you could create your own. Social networking sites make it easy to share information with others and enlist their support.

2. Build public support. Bring your positive message out to the streets of your neighborhood by gathering signatures on a petition in support of your cause. (One great online resource for petitions is www.ipetitions.com.) Put together a survey of questions to compile data on public attitudes about an issue.

3. Be aware of influential people who might not agree with your ideas. Building public support is crucial to advocacy efforts, but it's also important to contact people who have power to make high-level changes, including those who may have different views. Whether it's a public official or a company's CEO, try to engage important players and work together toward solutions.

4. Get the media involved. Work to get your message on TV, in newspapers, and on the radio by issuing press releases and inviting reporters to events. Media exposure can be an effective way to put pressure on decision makers.

5. Document your action. Film and take pictures of events that you participate in. You may be able to produce a public service announcement (PSA) or documentary that persuades others. Video pieces might include interviews with topic experts and supporters.

Protest

Protest can take many forms. You may immediately think of large rallies with thousands of people carrying signs and chanting slogans. This is one form of protest, but there are others. For example, you might refuse to buy goods or services from companies you believe are unethical.

The goal of protest is usually to achieve a change in law or policy—whether within a business, government agency, or another institution. Protest is often associated with riots or violence, perhaps because dramatic events are those most publicized. But the vast majority of demonstrations are non-violent. Most organizers realize that violence is counterproductive and frequently diminishes (rather than increases) public support for a cause.

A few ways you might protest include:

- attend a rally to voice your disapproval of public policy

- publicize a company's responsibility to clean up an environmental disaster

- raise your objections to a city regulation at a meeting of local officials

- take part in a sit-down, sit-in, stand-up, walk-out, or another act of dissent

- support a local agency working to address injustices

- refuse to buy clothing from a company that uses child labor

QUICK TIPS

Five Quick Protest Tips

1. If there are potential public safety issues, report events to police and other local officials. Look into any rules that may exist surrounding public protest. (For example, you may be allowed to protest only in designated areas.)

2. Be creative in getting attention. Perhaps you'll wear a symbolic costume or make a sign stating your beliefs. Brainstorm ideas for getting your message out there.

3. Use Web sites, instant messaging, and other networking tools to get the word out about your cause. You can also use these communication tools to organize and coordinate supporters on the day of an event.

4. Work to secure media coverage. News outlets are often especially interested when advocates for change are young people. If there are no cameras present, document the event on your own and consider making footage available at a social networking site.

5. Keep your cool. While passions may be strong about an issue, don't let conflicts or violence jeopardize the success of your event. If it does seem like things might get out of control, get the help of a public official.

Standing Up for Their Rights

Twenty-six middle school students whispered and nodded to one another, intent upon their conspiracy. It was 1901 in Wrzesnia, a small town in today's Poland. But at the turn of the 20th century, Poland had ceased to exist. It had been carved up by the European republics of Austria, Russia, and Prussia. In the Prussian region there was an attempt to abolish Polish identity, including forcing students to speak German at school. The conspiring students in Wrzesnia fought this order, demanding the right to speak Polish in their religion class. They protested by refusing to speak German, stomping their feet, drumming their knuckles on desks, and singing Polish songs.

Other students around the area learned about the strike and began their own protests. Over the next six years, the movement grew enormously, eventually leading to a general student strike of 93,000 students in 1907. The teens were often punished severely for their actions—including beatings, expulsions, fines, and a few imprisonments. Eventually these punishments quashed the strike. The students, however, did not entirely fail. Their story was published in newspapers everywhere and put the Polish fight for their native language, culture, and sovereignty in the world spotlight. It would take a decade, but world leaders remembered the plight of the Polish citizens and, following Prussian defeat in World War I, made it a condition for peace that Poland be re-created as a country.

Young people have played an important role protesting in countries around the world, including in the United States. Long before today's child labor laws, many children and teens worked in such places as coal mines and textile factories. Working conditions were sometimes dangerous in these places, and the compensation was low. To protest, the youth in America went on strike.

In 1836, for example, 11-year-old Harriet Hanson led 2,000 girls in a walkout of a Massachusetts mill, protesting for better working conditions. Agnes Nestor was 16 in 1897 when she helped lead the Garment Workers Strike in Chicago, Illinois. Also at the turn of the 20th century, a group of boys who were coal miners—some age 12 and younger—played an important role in getting workers more pay in Pennsylvanian coal mines.

In 1938, the Fair Labor Standards Act was passed. It protects young people in the United States from employment that is dangerous or infringes on their education.

When young people today rally for their rights, they do so while standing on the shoulders of many past giants.

4. Take Action

When you've decided on a cause, researched it, and determined your action, it's time to . . . well . . . act. Whether you're interested in volunteering, organizing people or resources, advocating for a cause, protesting, or another action, completing an action plan before getting started will be helpful. This plan can serve as a road map to help keep you moving forward.

Five-Step Action Plan

In getting ready for your action, write answers to the following questions. Be as detailed as possible. You will likely be able to use some of the information you compiled earlier (pages 12–13). Solid preparation is most often a crucial element of successful social action.

1. Write down your mission and goals. Think about what you want to accomplish with your action. Do you want to make a difference locally or have a global impact? What issue will you advocate for?

2. Decide how you will reach your goals. What actions will you take to make sure you accomplish your goals? This may include only a couple of steps or many.

3. Set a timeline for your action. When are you going to perform your service? Prioritize the steps you plan to take and create timelines for when you will take them.

4. Think about who will participate. Who can you include in your action? Friends and family members? Teachers and community leaders? People you worship with? Write down the names and contact information for those who can support and help your cause. (The next section, "Connecting with Others," has more information on joining or forming a youth organization.)

5. Plan out how you will draw attention to and (if necessary) raise funds for your cause. Will you be sending out a Public Service Announcement (PSA)? Conducting interviews or surveys? Fundraising? List the different ways you will get people to focus on and think about your action.

QUICK TIPS

Evaluating Your Progress

Keep questions like these in mind as you measure your progress toward goals.

1. What's working?
2. What's not?
3. Why am I having difficulties?
4. Is there a better course of action?
5. What changes should I make right now?

Connecting with Others

> *Together we can make a difference.*
> —Zach Hunter, 15, Global Activist

Why Work with a Group?

Working with a group can help you make a bigger impact for a cause. Larger numbers can give your movement more strength. Think of the aspen, a beautiful but fragile tree. The aspen's bark is thin and serves as a poor defense against disease and animals. But aspen trees hold a secret: Their roots connect underground in a common system. It is not unusual for an entire grove to consist of one root structure inherited from a common tree ancestor. When an aspen dies, it sends up new shoots. The strength of aspen trees, then, is in their connection. The same is true of groups—many people prove greater and stronger than one.

Should I Join a Group or Form My Own?

If you know you'd like to work for a cause with others, your next step will be to decide whether you want to join an existing organization or start a group of your own. There are benefits and potential pitfalls to both of these possibilities.

Questions to Consider

When you think about whether you'd like to join or form a group, it's important to consider a variety of factors. Here are some questions to keep in mind:

Benefits of Working with a Group

Working with a group and establishing connections with others allows you to:

➤ get diverse perspectives to understand an issue from all sides

➤ pool ideas and come up with creative solutions to problems

➤ capitalize on shared resources and networking opportunities

➤ use your numbers to add visibility and credibility to your position

➤ debate how to best move forward when difficulties arise

➤ develop friendships while increasing your impact

1. Are there groups already performing the action you'd like to participate in? If there are already many organizations devoted to a need, you might wish to join one of these groups so that you're not doubling up an effort. Why reinvent the wheel?

2. How strong is your commitment? Forming your own organization can require a great deal of energy and resources. Without plenty of both, you may not be effective in fighting for your cause. If you're not sure how strongly you want to get behind an effort, it's probably best to start off by joining a group whose work interests you.

3. What are the areas of greatest need? Is there a need in your community without proper advocates? If a problem is unaddressed, it might be a good time for you to start a group devoted to the issue.

4. Are you willing to lead for a cause? Some people have passion for a cause but don't necessarily want to lead or be in the spotlight. If this sounds like you, joining a group is likely a better option than creating one.

Joining a Group

Joining others on behalf of a cause can be very satisfying. You're functioning together as a team, each with your own responsibilities, doing important work. Established groups also have infrastructure, resources, and procedures that can allow you to make an immediate impact.

What Group Is Right for You?

When researching groups you might wish to join, keep these questions in mind:

1. What is the organization's mission? Consider carefully a group's mission and its methods for effecting change. You'll want an organization's purpose and ideals to match your own beliefs on an issue.

2. Are there any age requirements? Some organizations require you to be a certain age to participate unless a parent or legal guardian is also involved. Check on these rules as part of your research.

3. Are you looking for opportunities in your area or across the globe? Some groups offer many ways to take action at the local level. Others feature cultural exchanges, volunteer positions, conferences, and other opportunities to travel and serve abroad.

4. What kind of commitment is required? Maybe you're looking to volunteer locally for an hour or two each week. Perhaps you are ready to live in another nation for an extended period. Or your interests might be somewhere in between. Regardless, your commitment level will be an important factor in choosing an opportunity.

Youth Organizations

There are countless youth organizations located in every part of the world, with hundreds more being formed each year. It isn't possible to list every group involved in service and social action within a single book—and you might get bored reading it. But this section does include some of the largest organizations and youth networks operating today. You'll also find dozens of other groups appearing throughout this book.

Global Youth Action Network (GYAN)
www.youthlink.org
The Global Youth Action Network is one of the largest youth-led organizations on the planet. The network connects more than 10,000 network groups in over 180 countries. A "Guide to the Global Youth Movement," available on the site, compiles and lists these international groups of youth activists. GYAN also issues Global Youth Action Awards, helps coordinate Global Youth Service Day, and supports the effort to achieve the Millennium Development Goals (see page 24).

Point & Click

Millennium Development Goals
www.un.org/millenniumgoals
Many of the major youth organizations working at the global level are working toward the completion of the Millennium Development Goals (MDGs). These goals were established in 2000 at the United Nations Millennium Summit, a meeting of world powers to determine U.N. priorities for the 21st century. These are the objectives that international governments and organizations are working together to meet by 2015.

- Eradicate extreme poverty and hunger.
- Achieve universal primary education.
- Promote gender equality and empower women.
- Reduce child mortality.
- Improve maternal health.
- Combat HIV/AIDS, malaria, and other life-threatening diseases.
- Ensure environmental sustainability.
- Develop a global partnership for delivering aid.

The Millennium Development Goals cover a broad range of topics. To learn more about these world objectives, visit the Web site listed above.

TakingITGlobal
www.takingitglobal.org
TakingITGlobal involves youth in positive change in more than 200 countries. A key part of what the organization does is to promote technology as a means of connecting people to address the earth's challenges. The Web site does just this—serving as a directory of youth organizations, a reference guide for understanding major issues, and a place to communicate (via blogs and message boards) with others effecting positive change.

Free the Children
www.freethechildren.com
Free the Children is one of the world's largest networks of young people. More than one million children and teens have been involved in the network's education and development programs in over 45 countries. Founded by youth activist Craig Kielburger (see pages 10–11), the organization has sent more than nine million dollars of medical supplies to clinics around the world. Visit the Web site to learn how you can help supply schools, fund sanitation, invest in small businesses, and much more.

Oxfam International
www.oxfam.org
Oxfam International is a confederation of 13 organizations working together with over 3,000 partners in more than 100 countries to find lasting solutions to poverty,

disease, and other global concerns. Two programs the organization sponsors are Oxfam International Youth Partnerships and Youth Parliament (www.iyp.oxfam. org/connect)—a global network of young leaders and activists working for sustainable living.

Youth Venture
www.genv.net
Youth Venture helps teams of people start new youth-led organizations. The group has offices in many countries around the world. Visit the Web site to join in social-action forums and find tools for starting your own group, including an interactive action plan.

YouthNoise
www.youthnoise.com
YouthNoise is an online youth community that offers young people a chance to speak out and take action on many issues. Log on to take surveys, voice your opinion, make one-click contributions, and track down service opportunities.

National Youth Leadership Council
www.nylc.org
The National Youth Leadership Council brings together the service learning field at the National

Service-Learning Conference, which attracts young people from all 50 states and dozens of other countries. Youth give demonstrations of projects for adults and other youth involved in service. The organization's Web site offers hands-on tools, descriptions of projects, service articles, and more.

YMCA International
www.ymca.net/international
Programs through YMCA International involve 45 million people in 120 nations. The organization works with youth and families to promote strong, safe, and healthy communities. You might get involved by attending a leadership camp, performing service in the community, participating in a cultural exchange, or one of many other available opportunities. You can log on to the Web site for more information or visit a location near you.

World YWCA
www.worldywca.info

Founded in 1855, the YWCA is one of the oldest and largest organizations in the world working for gender equity. Its programs help over 25 million women and girls in 125 countries and support other social movements for human rights and peace. You can go online to find a listing of YWCA programs by country as well as current information on the group's health, social justice, and humanitarian efforts.

Point & Click

Most of the organizations in this section have a global presence. To learn more about regional groups involved in service and social action, visit the following Web sites.

Latin American Youth Forum
www.orgs.takingitglobal.org/4709

Asian Youth Council
www.asiayouth.org

South African Youth Council
www.sayc.org.za

European Youth Forum
www.youthforum.org

Pacific Youth Council
www.spc.int/youth/PYC/pacific_youth_council.htm

Youth Service America (YSA)
www.ysa.org

Youth Service America engages millions of young people in service to their communities in the United States and more than 100 other countries. YSA is a primary sponsor of Global Youth Service Day, the largest celebration of youth service around the world, and offers grants, tools, and resources to support youth-led service projects year-round. Log on to the Web site for more information and a link to SERVEnet, a resource for finding volunteer opportunities near you.

Boys and Girls Clubs of America
www.bgca.org

If you're interested in making your neighborhood a better place for young people, consider getting involved in a program from the Boys and Girls Clubs of America. The organization, with affiliates in hundreds of communities around the United States, features character and leadership initiatives, sports and recreation opportunities, and arts and life skills programs. The Web site can help you find locations near you.

World Assembly of Youth
www.way.org.my

This global network connects national youth councils and organizations from every region of the world. In all, the World Assembly of Youth unites the efforts of 110 member organizations from all continents. The group also serves as an advisor and advocate on youth issues at the United Nations. Log on to the Web site to learn about local groups that are part of the network addressing such issues as human rights, youth representation, health, and community development.

Big Brothers Big Sisters International (BBBSI)
www.bbbsi.org

Big Brothers Big Sisters International connects young people at-risk with positive role models. The group has affiliates all around the world that offer one-on-one mentoring, internships, and other opportunities to get involved in the community. The Web site lists positions, locations, and steps you can take to participate.

Peace Child International
www.peacechild.org

Headquartered in the United Kingdom, Peace Child International empowers young people to work for peace, human rights, and environmental initiatives. Education and leadership opportunities are included in programs, as are opportunities to produce publications and attend the World Youth Congress, a semi-annual forum on the role of youth in achieving the U.N. Millennium Development Goals.

One World Youth Project
www.oneworldyouthproject.org

This organization has a program for middle and high school students in the United States and Canada that pairs up students with peers from around the world. The program emphasizes joint community-service ventures in support of the U.N. Millennium Development Goals.

International Youth Foundation
www.iyfnet.org

International Youth Foundation works with corporations and global affiliates in nearly 70 nations and regions to provide young people with education opportunities. Programs focus on positive health, technology training, leadership, and other skills young people can use to get jobs and improve their lives. Visit the organization online to find out how you can help in this effort.

International Association for National Youth Service (IANYS)
www.ianys.utas.edu.au
The International Association for National Youth Service, operating for over 15 years, connects youth organizations in Europe, Australasia, North America, and Africa. Log on to the Web site to find global partners, join online forums, and learn about conference opportunities.

DIFFERENCE MAKER

Benjamin Quinto

Global Youth Action Network (GYAN) is one of the world's largest youth networks. But would you believe the group was borne of disappointment? Benjamin Quinto, a New York City teen, thought a lot about global problems and how they affected young people: "I wondered what kind of world this was where every day 35,000 children die around the world because of hunger and disease and other preventable things."

Instead of giving up, however, Ben decided to make things happen. He saw youth representation at the United Nations as a way to help reduce global tragedies and attended a meeting with a friend who was involved in the organization. "But when I arrived at the U.N., I looked around the meeting at all the delegates there. I asked myself, 'Where are all the young people?' I was the youngest person there." Ben spent the following three years trying to establish a youth assembly with the United Nations. Proposal after proposal was denied, however, and Ben realized the large bureaucracy was not ready for change.

But Ben's effort at the U.N. was not a waste of time. Through his work with the organization, Ben became familiar with the activism of young people everywhere. "Then I realized there was a whole global youth movement already out there," says Ben. "We just needed to organize and to network. Although there were amazing youth actions all over the world, they were not connected." To address this, Ben and some friends set up the United Youth Conference in 1999 in Sedona, Arizona. Participants from 12 countries took part. Their goal: unite the socially active youth around the globe. High on their list of priorities was creating a Web site where young people could network with one another. The site would also provide those who were new to activism with information for getting involved.

Six months after the conference, Ben and his supporters opened up the Global Youth Action Network office, ironically, only one block from the United Nations in New York City. The network, after such a short time, already represented 110 countries. The group's Web site also went online, connecting difference makers around the world. Over the following few years, GYAN was able to establish regional groups and offices across the globe. They continued to expand their reach and today connect more than 10,000 network groups in over 180 countries. GYAN and its sister group—TakingItGlobal—have succeeded in mobilizing millions of youth in social action.

It's probably a good thing that Global Youth Action Network is based so close to the United Nations. In 2005, after building relationships with the U.N. over the course of four years, GYAN was granted "special consultative status" with the U.N. Economic and Social Council. That means the group must be invited to meetings at which issues affecting youth (such as poverty relief and gender equality) are discussed. Ben's efforts have come full circle, and young people everywhere have stronger representation at the United Nations.

Forming a Group

What if you believe your service or action requires forming your own group? Starting an organization can be one of the most satisfying things you ever do. It may even become your life's work and passion.

Five-Step Action Plan

1. Gather members for your group. Recruit classmates, family members, teachers, or community leaders for your cause. You may decide to also seek the backing of area groups. You might build support online by creating a Web site or setting up a personal page for your cause at a social-networking site. Where you look for support, how many people you include, and what partnerships you seek out will depend a lot upon the scope of your project.

2. Set up a meeting. You might plan to hold meetings in your home or—with permission from the appropriate official—at school or another place in the community. If you have mainly online support, you may need to set up a Web conference so that everyone can stay involved and up to date on your group's action.

3. Settle on a name for your group, a mission statement, and goals. What will your organization be called? What is your mission? How do you plan to achieve it?

4. Create an action plan for carrying out your organization's work. Your action plan should include your group's mission and goals, the steps you will take to accomplish them, a timeline of group events, and a listing of roles (who will do what and when).

5. Plan for publicity and fundraising efforts. Public attention can help you build momentum for your cause. You may also need to raise funds for materials, travel, or other operating expenses. Be sure to include in your action plan what steps you will take to publicize and fund your organization.

Point & Click

Idealist—Nonprofit FAQ
www.idealist.org/npofaq
You might wish to file for status as a nonprofit organization. The application process for doing this can vary a great deal by country, state, province, or region. This Web site is an informative and helpful resource for getting information on the process.

Human Rights

 We are the someone, and today is the day. **99**
—Zach Hunter, 15, Global Activist

What Are the Facts?

History is full of events that denied people their human rights. The issue is complicated because cultures and nations often have differing perspectives on what humans' basic rights are. After the atrocities of the Holocaust were fully known, the United Nations addressed this problem by drafting the Universal Declaration of Human Rights. This document pledged that all people have the right to equality, health, and freedom of thought, expression, and movement—regardless of a person's race, gender, religion, political affiliation, or cultural beliefs.

By The Numbers

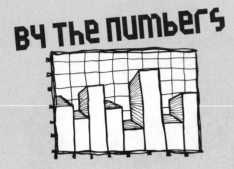

Human Rights:

➤ Currently, an estimated 27 million people are enslaved around the world. (Free the Slaves, www.freetheslaves.net)

➤ Sex-trade trafficking is a $7 billion business worldwide each year. (International Organisation for Migration, www.iom.int)

➤ Worldwide, one in three women has been beaten, coerced into sex, or abused in some other way. (United Nations Population Fund, www.unfpa.org)

➤ More than 200 million children worldwide are engaged in child labor—destructive to their mental, physical, and emotional development. (International Labour Organization, www.ilo.org)

➤ Three out of four people killed in the world's current wars are women and children. (Network for Good, www.networkforgood.org)

Since being adopted by U.N. member countries in 1948, the Universal Declaration of Human Rights has served as the standard by which people must be treated. Unfortunately, it has not prevented countless human-rights violations, and many continue today.

War, poverty, cultural conflict, and abuse of power all increase the possibility of human-rights abuses occurring within or between countries or regions of the world. Unfortunately, abuses can continue undetected for long periods of time. When they are known, delayed or limited reaction by outside countries often allows conditions to continue or get worse. Many of those responsible for crimes are never held to account for their acts against humanity.

The positive news is that progress on protecting human rights has been made by such monumental figures as Gandhi, Martin Luther King Jr., Mother Teresa, Nelson Mandela, Jimmy Carter, Eleanor Roosevelt, and Kofi Annan. New technologies also allow for greater awareness of abuses and improved communication and coordination among those advocating on behalf of oppressed people. This section offers many ways you can join in the campaign for human rights.

Keep It Local

Investigate and report on community injustices. Some people hear "human rights abuses" and they think of faraway nations. In fact, the violation of a person's rights can occur in any place or at any time. For example, some people believe discrimination in the United States continues to limit full participation in the government and economy by cultural, ethnic, and religious minorities. Following are a few ways you can make a difference.

- Research issues affecting people in your area. Maybe you've learned of a group or person being discriminated against or denied full legal rights. Local media outlets, online forums, newspapers, and your neighborhood library are all good places to start looking for information.

- Choose venues to spread your message of equality. Consider posting your views on a current-affairs blog or social-networking site. You might also conduct an email campaign to make the public aware of human-rights violations and to lobby officials who make decisions on policies.

- Set up public events to raise awareness about injustices. You could work with teachers to organize an assembly at your school or set up a public demonstration in a plaza. Also consider boycotting businesses that do not support equal opportunity.

- Meet people with influence whose decisions will affect the outcome of an issue. These people might include business leaders, council members, or members of advocacy groups working on behalf of people being denied rights.

Point & Click

United Nations Human Rights Web Page
www.un.org/rights
To learn more, check out this Web site from the U.N. on human rights. You'll find links to the Universal Declaration of Human Rights, information on Human Rights Day (December 10), and suggestions for taking action against abuses.

Convention on the Rights of the Child
www.unicef.org
The Convention on the Rights of the Child, issued by the U.N. in 1990, states that young people have some undeniable rights. These include the right to:

- life
- name and identity
- guardians who are free to exercise parental responsibilities
- protection, a home, education, and basic needs
- express opinions and have them heard and considered
- protection from abuse or exploitation
- protection of privacy
- representation and defense in any court
- ineligibility for capital punishment

DIFFERENCE MAKER

Cindy Perez

Cindy Perez knows a lot about the fight for equal rights. As a high school student, Cindy learned that many immigrants who were not yet citizens in her state of Kansas were ineligible to attend its colleges or universities. She immediately decided to do something about it. Working from her home base in Olathe, Cindy circulated a petition, spoke before Kansas lawmakers, and helped prepare a documentary that profiled the lives of immigrant students. All of these actions were important toward passage of the DREAM Act—the Development, Relief, and Education for Alien Minors Act—legislation enacted in 2004 that ensures higher education opportunities for immigrant children, including those still on their path to citizenship.

Cindy understands well the immigrant experience. She arrived in Olathe with her parents when she was in second grade. At the time, she thought she was on a visit to see her father and that the family would return to their home near Chihuahua, Mexico. It eventually became clear, though, that the family would stay in the United States. Things in her new home were not always easy. She initially had challenges learning English and keeping up with the other students at her new school. Only through a lot of hard work she was able to catch up. But when she did, Cindy refused to sit back and relax. Instead, she kept studying until she was one of the top performers in her class. Cindy knew a lot of the other immigrants in her area were like her—smart and hard-working people who just wanted a chance to make their lives better. That's why getting the DREAM Act passed was so important to her.

Cindy knows that the struggle for equal opportunity is ongoing. To continue progress she has worked with her school and local government to develop additional immigrant programs designed to help them succeed. She wants to be sure others have the opportunities she's enjoyed. And the DREAM Act—well, it may soon apply beyond the state of Kansas. Cindy has worked with U.S. senators in an effort to expand it to the federal level. And only time will tell the full impact she has in advancing equality.

Connect

Platform for International Cooperation on Undocumented Migrants
www.picum.org
Immigration is sometimes a sensitive issue because people worry that an infusion of immigrants will dilute a nation's financial resources, culture, or identity. This is a growing problem in European nations where record numbers of immigrants are causing resentment among many. This organization advocates for immigrants in Europe (for health care benefits, housing, and other basic rights) while also promoting social harmony. Log on to the group's site to learn more about programs and how you can help.

U.S. Citizenship and Immigration Services
www.uscis.gov
This Web site from the U.S. government outlines immigration laws and regulations, gives information on securing services and benefits, and features forms, links, and other tools for people new to the country. You can monitor equal opportunity legislation in the United States and find links for writing to representatives at www.congress.org. If you live in Canada, go to www.canada.gc.ca for links to government officials.

Become an advocate for your rights—and those of other young people around the world. Unfortunately, the U.N. Convention on the Rights of the Child has not prevented many abuses. For example, child labor and human trafficking are booming businesses in many regions. How can you advocate for the rights of young people everywhere?

- Help provide food, shelter, and other needs for young people. In every country, some children go without the basic necessities called for in the Convention on the Rights of the Child. Contact local charities to find out how you can help in your city, village, or borough.

- Connect with a national or an international group working on behalf of children. Consider organizing a local drive or fundraiser to collect goods or resources for this organization. For example, you could raise funds for a group working to release children in bonded labor.

Advocate for the rights of women. In some countries, cultures, and religions, women are thought to be inferior to men. This can lead to many injustices—including limited educational opportunities, denial of political representation, trafficking, and other terrible crimes. What can you do?

- Help stop human trafficking. Human trafficking takes place in virtually every nation of the world. Women and children make up the majority of people who are trafficked. They are often the victims of abuse and forced to become sex workers. Research this problem and learn how you can become an advocate by visiting www. humantrafficking.org, an online

resource with actions you can take no matter where you live.

- Help end female genital mutilation. Female genital mutilation (sometimes called "female circumcision") includes removal of or damage to the female genitalia. Often performed for cultural or religious reasons, the practice causes intense pain and long-lasting physical and emotional effects. According to the World Health Organization, at least 100 million girls and women are victims of female genital mutilation, with another two million at risk each year. Find out how you can help by visiting the Web site of the Female Genital Cutting Education and Networking Project (www.fgmnetwork.org).

- Speak out against violence and sexual abuse. Whether physical, verbal, or emotional, abuse has long-lasting effects on a person. Women are most often the victims of abuse, and many remain silent about it because they are afraid of the offender, often a partner. Not only a concern for adults, rape and dating violence is also on the rise among teens. Do your part to address these trends. You might volunteer with a local crisis center that helps people escape abusers or start a schoolwide campaign to bring awareness to violence and sexual assault against women.

Florence Nabayinda Babumba

Florence Nabayinda Babumba remembers hot nights sleeping on the ground, coughing and fighting her way through malaria, measles, flu, and strange fevers brought on by insect bites. Labeled "retarded," Florence was abandoned by her mother and beaten and neglected by her father. Others in Masaka, her Ugandan village, often were no kinder. The headmaster at her school called Florence "useless" and told her many times she should drop out of school because she was "unteachable."

"I felt like complete trash," says Florence. She was treated badly by many of the people around her— all because she was a girl who was intellectually disabled.

Sometimes Florence could see the humps of the Rwenzori Mountains in the distance. Their peaks stretched into the sky, far above the troubles on Earth. Florence wished she could also rise above the Earth—that she could fly high above her problems.

Things changed for Florence when she was 14. Her father's stepbrother adopted her. Her new family loved and supported Florence in ways she'd never experienced. Her adopted father insisted she further her education. This meant attending class with seven-year-old children, children who teased her for being so far behind. It wasn't easy, but Florence persisted and made progress.

Florence received another chance when her adopted father formed a Ugandan chapter of the Special Olympics. He challenged Florence to compete in racing. Dashing along dirt paths on long, slim legs, Florence ran through mangrove forests and past shy sugarbirds. With each mile her legs and lungs grew stronger. She began competing in races and winning medals in Africa and across the globe. Florence's accomplishments gained her a lot of attention—including from world leaders.

In her new life, Florence gained strength and dignity, but she remembered how she felt being called "stupid" and "retarded." Realizing that many people with disabilities continued to be denied their rights, Florence started a campaign to help them. She began by speaking at 45 Special Olympics districts about the need for better education opportunities for girls, especially those who had intellectual disabilities. But it wasn't until she wrote to (and eventually met) the queen of Buganda, a large district in southeast Uganda, that true action began to happen. In part due to Florence's lobbying, the queen established a foundation for children in need. She and the king also put into effect the Universal Primary Education requirement—a law that requires children be allowed to go to school, regardless of gender or disability. No longer could children be sent home because they were "unteachable."

Florence hung up her training shoes after 12 years of competition, but she plans to keep running—maybe this time for office. Currently a board member for the Special Olympics, Florence hopes to one day serve in the Ugandan Parliament where she plans to continue to advocate for intellectually disabled children.

Florence now gazes into the distance at the snow-capped peaks of the Rwenzori Mountains. She smiles broadly and throws her fist triumphantly into the air.

Connect

Special Olympics International
www.specialolympics.org
Special Olympics is about a lot more than athletics. The organization works to empower people who have intellectual disabilities to be not only physically fit, but also respected and important members of society. Working on an international level, the group serves more than one million people in over 150 countries. Log on to the site to learn how you can get involved.

Promote the safety and care of elders. Did you know it's estimated that more than one million seniors in the United States are abused, neglected, or otherwise mistreated by people responsible for their care? Elder abuse is an international problem, and there are many organizations working to help eliminate it. You can learn how to become an advocate by visiting the Web site of the National Center on Elder Abuse (www.elderabusecenter.org) or the International Network for the Prevention of Elder Abuse (www.inpea.net). Another excellent way to support elders' care is to volunteer at a local senior center.

Take It Global

Work to abolish slavery and other illegal labor practices. Slavery is one of the most pressing human-rights concerns today. *Bonded labor* is one way in which people are enslaved or trafficked. Many children and teens are affected when their parents, unable to pay a debt, are forced to give them up to be laborers. These young people are often forced to work in factories or the sex trade, or to fight as child soldiers in armed conflicts. What can you do to help end these and other atrocities?

- Read about and speak out against human-rights violations. Research abuses that concern you and work to get your opinion heard by others. You might send a letter to the editor of a newspaper or outline your positions in current-events chatrooms. Think about using your research to write an article and submit it for publication in a local or national journal.

- Start a campaign against child labor. Millions of children around the world work legally to help support their families. There is often nothing wrong with this if employment does not harm the child's health or education and the child is fairly compensated. Millions of other young people, however, are forced to work (virtually as slaves) in jobs that are dangerous and offer insufficient pay (or none at all). People often don't realize their own buying habits may support this practice. Consider setting up an information campaign to inform consumers of this situation. One target you could consider is a company that sells goods produced by child labor. You might distribute flyers with information about illegal labor practices to shoppers, send mass emails to those who might be interested in supporting your boycott, or post comments on a consumer-reports blog.

Connect

OneWorld.net
www.oneworld.net
OneWorld is an online media network of 10 countries and regions that offers comprehensive international news on human-rights issues. Based in the United Kingdom, the network also has centers operating in Africa, the Netherlands, Canada, Latin America, Austria, Italy, Finland, South Asia, the United States, and Spain. At the site, you'll find stories (including articles, sound recordings, photo essays, and video footage) from all over the world and have the opportunity to contribute your feedback on important issues.

Stop Child Labor
www.stopchildlabor.org
Visit this site to stay informed about international child labor. You'll find information you can use to avoid supporting companies whose values don't align with yours. You can also express your opinions in an online forum and read updates on efforts to protect minors from dangerous and demeaning work.

Coalition to Stop the Use of Child Soldiers
www.child-soldiers.org
In many regions of the world, children are forced to fight as soldiers in combat. This problem most often occurs in developing nations experiencing civil wars or ethnic conflicts. The Coalition to Stop the Use of Child Soldiers updates Web visitors on what's happening where and offers opportunities to help stop atrocities.

- Monitor foreign policy. Did you know that many governments form political or economic partnerships with pretty much any country—even if a nation has an awful record on human rights? Many human-rights activists believe this to be implicit support of violations. If you agree, check up on how your government is dealing with some of the top human-rights offenders. If you don't like what you find out, voice your disapproval to officials, newspapers, and online forums.

Fundraise on behalf of an organization devoted to human rights. Many government agencies and nonprofit organizations are working to address human-rights concerns around the globe. If you'd like to make a difference in the effort against injustice, consider raising funds for one of these groups. Every contribution—no matter what amount—is appreciated and welcome. There are many possible ways to fundraise.

- Hold a benefit dinner. Make sure that you advertise your cause and inform people where contributions will be spent. You might hold the dinner at your school or place of worship, a community hall, or another local setting. Arrange for entertainment, games, and other attractions to ensure your event draws as many people as possible.

- Organize a battle of the bands. If you like music, a concert for human rights might be a good fit for you. Ask friends to play and recruit talent from the local scene for a battle of the bands—a competition between different musical groups. Search for a venue that will host the event for free, and solicit donations from attendees. Make sure to spread the word about the event at school and in the community.

- Organize a fundraiser. You might, for example, pledge to complete a long bike ride, run, or kayak trip in exchange for donations. Plan an event or trip, and ask family members, friends, and neighbors for pledges of support. Check with any organizations you're affiliated with (such as scouts) to see whether they will sponsor you.

Connect

Amnesty International
www.amnesty.org
Amnesty International is one of the largest human-rights organizations. Independent of all governments, the organization networks over two million people who are addressing abuses all over the globe. The group's Web site has current information on where atrocities are occurring and what you can do to help end them.

Human Rights Watch
www.hrw.org
Human Rights Watch monitors abuses occurring around the world and mobilizes activists against them. The Web site provides current reports on concerns ranging from refugee crises to women's rights violations, and it gives suggestions for actions you can take.

DIFFERENCE MAKER

Wojciech Gryc

One night in 2003, 15-year-old Wojciech Gryc received a call that would change his life forever. It was right around midnight, and Wojciech wondered who could be calling. It was the highway patrol with terrible news—his sister, Magdalena, had been struck and killed by a motorist. The news was devastating. Wojciech and his older sister had been close. After immigrating with their parents from Bialystok, Poland, the siblings had relied on each other in their new home in Ontario, Canada.

Wojciech realized he couldn't bring back his sister. He did wonder, though, if there was something he could do, something positive to honor her. "This is when I began Five Minutes to Midnight, an online newspaper," Wojciech says. "I chose to focus on human rights."

It was 2003 and Wojciech spent many late nights pounding the keys of his computer. Surrounded by stacks of books, he wrote about crippling poverty, devastating diseases, and other events—including the war that had recently begun in Iraq. Wojciech asked tough questions and recruited the help of high school friends. To get varying perspectives and firsthand accounts, he solicited contributions from other young people around the world.

Five Minutes to Midnight's subscription list has grown steadily. Wojciech's articles (and those of other contributors) have been picked up by many other publications. An anthology of these stories is available, and the proceeds support youth-focused organizations. Five Minutes to Midnight volunteers also represent the group at important events like the World Urban Forum and the International AIDS Conference. Wojciech has transformed Five Minutes to Midnight from a tiny newspaper into a far-reaching youth organization that connects teens from all over the world and organizes international projects.

Connect

Five Minutes to Midnight
www.fiveminutestomidnight.org
Wojciech Gryc's organization helps inform young people on human-rights issues and current affairs. The goal is to promote critical thinking about the world's problems and involve other youth in solving them. The group offers media awareness training, leadership programs, and involvement in international projects. Visit the site to learn how you can volunteer with the organization as a correspondent, Web developer, or another position.

Serve as a student ambassador. Would you like to take a service trip? There are many youth organizations offering volunteer opportunities around the planet. Commitments can range from one week to one year (or more). When checking out opportunities, be sure to keep in mind age requirements, expenses, and the commitment level required. Following are a few programs where you can start looking. Many others can be found in "Connecting with Others" (pages 21–30) and throughout the book.

Youth at the United Nations
www.un.org/youth
The United Nations is one of the most important institutions in the world. It develops partnerships between countries, works for global human-rights initiatives, and unites aid efforts. Visit the U.N. for information on pressing human-rights concerns facing our world and what can be done to help. You can also learn how to become a youth delegate and use the opportunity to advocate for human rights at the United Nations General Assembly.

One World Youth Project
www.oneworldyouthproject.org
Want to experience another culture while also working to accomplish the U.N. Millennium Development Goals? An exchange through One World Youth Project may be right for you. Go to the organization's Web site to learn where opportunities are and how you can get involved. You'll also find current news and blogs from ambassadors already out in the world.

Voices of Youth (UNICEF)
www.unicef.org/voy
UNICEF is a program of the United Nations that advocates for the rights and welfare of children around the world. The Web site serves as a clearinghouse of information on ways you can support international causes or how to begin a project of your own. Log on the site for practical information as well as opportunities for traveling to the Junior 8 Summit. This is a program that allows youth to be represented at the G8 Summit, an annual meeting of the world's wealthiest countries.

DIFFERENCE MAKER

Zach Hunter

When Zach Hunter learned that there are people working as slaves in the 21st century, he was shocked. Zach was 12 at the time. His fifth-grade class at Christian Fellowship School in Ashburn, Virginia, was studying Harriet Tubman and Frederick Douglass during Black History Month when his mom mentioned that many people continue to live as slaves today. In fact, he learned that there are about 27 million people forced to work in mills, factories, and brothels around the world—half of whom are women and children.

Zach immediately knew he had to do something to help. What did he do? He started collecting money to support organizations dedicated to ending modern-day slavery. But he didn't request huge checks or $100 bills. Instead, he asked people for the loose change they had in their homes, cars, and pockets. Zach's idea caught on, and it wasn't long before others in his school started collecting. There was such a sensation over the cause that teens in other schools all over the United States began piling up pennies, nickels, quarters, and dimes on behalf of the cause. Zach named the campaign "Loose Change to Loosen Chains." It has, to date, raised thousands and thousands of dollars to free slaves around the world. And it continues to gain momentum.

Today, Zach speaks at high schools, places of worship, and other community meeting places around the United States. In fact, Zach will talk about ending modern-day slavery with pretty much anyone who will listen. And his commitment is, quite literally, paying off. Young people around the country are picking up the campaign's signature yellow cup and collecting coins to end slavery—all inspired by Zach's message about who can make a difference: "We are the someone, and today is the day."

Connect

Loose Change to Loosen Chains
www.lc2lc.org
Visit the Web site of Loose Change to Loosen Chains to learn more about Zach and how you can begin collecting in the effort to abolish slavery.

Hunger and Homelessness

 The world is not perfect, and it's up to those who have the ability—the resources and the support system—to change things.
—Mihiri Tillakaratne, 18, Global Activist

What Are the Facts?

Homelessness and hunger are global challenges. There are people everywhere who do not have adequate food or shelter. You may be aware of families in need in your own town or neighborhood. You've probably also seen media reports on other areas affected by starvation and homelessness, including those affected by drought or natural disasters.

BY THE NUMBERS

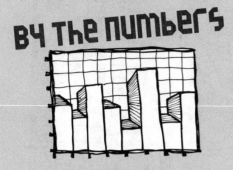

Hunger and Homelessness:

➤ About 850 million people worldwide are hungry. (World Food Programme, www.wfp.org)

➤ Almost 16,000 children die each day from hunger-related causes—or one child every five seconds. (Bread for the World, www.bread.org)

➤ Of two billion children on the planet, 640 million—or about one in three—live without proper shelter. (UNICEF, www.unicef.org)

➤ About 750,000 people experience homelessness every night in the United States. Only about half are accepted into shelters. (U.S. Department of Housing and Urban Development, www.hud.gov)

➤ In the world's wealthiest countries, one out of every six children lives in relative poverty (less than half of a nation's median income). (UNICEF, www.unicef.org)

➤ About 14 million children in the United States face hunger on a daily basis. (Society of Saint Andrew, www.endhunger.org)

While significantly affecting all nations, hunger and homelessness are often more severe and widespread in developing nations. Areas of the world most in need of assistance include regions of Asia, Africa, Central Europe, and Latin America. The reasons underlying extreme poverty are often complex. Limited economic development, war, disease, overpopulation, poor governance, and environmental events can all be factors. For years, many aid organizations have devoted resources toward ending global poverty. Still, much work remains to be done.

In addition to being threatened by starvation or exposure, people living in poverty often suffer psychological stress from constant concern about their welfare. They are also, disproportionately, victims of human trafficking, violence, abuse, illegal labor, and other human-rights violations. Children are the most affected by these dangers. They may be forced to fight as soldiers, work with dangerous machinery and equipment, or engage in prostitution. In these desperate situations, educational opportunities are intentionally severely limited so that exploitation can continue indefinitely. This section offers ways you can address poverty locally and around the world.

Keep It Local

Volunteer with a community agency that helps people in need. Search online or in city publications (such as a phone book) for food banks or shelters in your area. Outreach opportunities are often also available through faith groups, schools, and other community agencies. If you're having trouble finding the right place to help, visit Do Something (www.dosomething.org), a Web site with information on hunger and homelessness projects around the world.

Organize an effort to collect items for those in need. You might ask the public for donations of nonperishable food, blankets, clothing (including winter items like hats, coats, and gloves), toys, and any other supplies that can be distributed to local families. Consider involving your school, house of worship, or another organization you're involved in. You can get a collection under way with these simple steps.

- Research community needs. Contact agencies addressing hunger and homelessness in your area and ask what items are needed. Also discuss the logistics of distributing donations once an effort is complete.
- Collaborate with public officials, school staff, and local businesspeople to create drop-off spots around your town or neighborhood. Ask these people to consider being collection sponsors.

- Advertise your campaign. Ask newspapers, TV and radio stations, and Web sites to promote your cause. You might create a public service announcement (PSA) that details drop-off locations, hours, and destinations where donated goods will go. Putting up posters or handing out flyers in public areas are also good options for letting others know about your drive.
- Connect your campaign to special events or days on the calendar. Food and gift drives, for example, commonly occur around holidays. You might also conduct your campaign during a village or city festival when many people are out in support of the community.

DIFFERENCE MAKER

Ilona Seure

Ilona Seure knew she wanted to help others—how and where, though, she wasn't sure about at first. Her work eventually would be with children in her native Amsterdam—capital of the Netherlands. Ilona works with some of the estimated 10,000 young people who are homeless in her nation.

Ilona works through Don Bosco, an international service organization that reconnects youth with the community through friendship and life-skills activities. This might mean attending education gatherings, visiting a museum, or just spending time together. Because many who are homeless feel isolated and separated from society, the program pairs teens with mentors like Ilona, and gives them the opportunity to share their experiences and make new friends. When kids who are homeless begin to establish a social network within the community, transitioning to a more stable life becomes easier.

What inspired Ilona to help youth in need? It was a trip to Vijayawade, India, in 2003. In the city of one million people, many children didn't have adults who could provide for them and had little choice but to live in the streets. Seventeen-year-old Ilona saw that she could make a difference in their lives. She spent time with the children, taught them life skills, and played the role of big sister. Her experience taught her that making a difference often means more than donating goods or money for a cause—it's about connecting with others and expressing genuine care for them.

Back in Amsterdam, this lesson still serves Ilona well. She is building relationships with teens who once believed they were from different worlds. And those once "lost" to the streets are becoming part of the community—something that makes it a better place for all who live there.

Connect

Don Bosco Youth Net
www.donboscoyouth.net
Don Bosco youth organizations operate with offices in a dozen countries that include Malta, Argentina, Italy, the United Kingdom, and Slovenia. The group operates exchanges designed to support youth in many areas of the world. Visit the Web site to learn about opportunities.

Advocate for people who are hungry or homeless. Some believe that people in need are "lazy" or just need to "get to work." Poverty is actually a very complex issue that can't be explained by such simplistic (and biased) language. Consider researching hunger and homelessness—its causes and consequences—and becoming an advocate for those affected. Following are a couple ways you can get involved.

- Create a PSA about poverty in your area. Interview local experts on the topic and share what you learn with others. Raise awareness using flyers, posters, PSAs, and video sharing. You might also express your views in newspapers (with a letter to the editor), at online news sites, or on a personal blog.

CARE

www.care.org

To advocate for a cause, you need to know a lot about it. CARE is one organization you can visit online for data on global poverty as well as ideas for taking action. CARE has offices in over 30 nations and operates campaigns in some of Earth's poorest regions. You can visit the Web site to read special reports, view video, and become a volunteer.

Food Research and Action Center

www.frac.org

Where can you find information on hunger in the United States? One good source is the Food Research and Action Center, an advocacy group promoting public policy to end hunger. At the Web site you'll find a lot of statistics on hunger and information on pending legislative action and federal food programs. You can also check out the group's many publications, sign up for a newsletter, or act in the Campaign to End Childhood Hunger.

National Alliance to End Homelessness

www.endhomelessness.org

This organization advocates on behalf of people who are homeless in the United States. The Web site offers research on homelessness, including policy recommendations. Log on to learn more about those affected by this problem and what you can do to help solve it.

- You might join the ONE Campaign (www.one.org) against global poverty. Taking action against hunger and homelessness in your area is great. But you can also make a difference across the world—without traveling far from home. You can log on to the Web site to sign the ONE Declaration, a demand for world leaders to make helping people in need a priority. You'll also find ideas for spreading the word to others about the campaign.

Join the effort to provide housing for all.
Are you the type of person who doesn't mind rolling up your sleeves to get a job done? Then you might be a perfect candidate to help build homes for others. There are a number of programs that work to house families. To find the right opportunity for you, contact a local service agency or an international organization involved in the effort to put roofs over the heads of people who need one.

UN-HABITAT
www.unhabitat.org
With a mission of "shelter for all," UN-HABITAT works to help supply the world's people with housing. A primary focus of the global organization is the developing world where many people live in urban slums and shantytowns. UN-HABITAT advocates for proper city planning, clean water and sanitation projects, environmental sustainability, and affordable housing opportunities. Log on to the Web site to learn about programs.

Habitat for Humanity
www.habitat.org
Habitat for Humanity builds homes all over the world. While you must be 16 to help on building sites, there are a number of other ways for younger kids to get involved through the Youth United program (www.habitat.org/youthprograms). These positions include planning, fundraising, and serving as a liaison to the public. The great thing about Habitat for Humanity is that you can help in so many different areas—close to home or around the world.

DIFFERENCE MAKER

William and Patrick Stoudt

What do you do when a hurricane levels your neighborhood? If you're William or Patrick Stoudt, you get to work. In 2005, after Hurricane Katrina caused much of New Orleans, Louisiana, to be a flooded mess, the twin Stoudt brothers sprang into action. "Our house looked like a bomb had gone off," reported William. He and Patrick, though, refused to give up on their community. Instead, they recruited their buddy Wade Trosclair and started Youth Rebuilding New Orleans (www.yrno.org).

With the help of other young people from their high school, the boys have performed cleanup operations around the city. They've picked up debris, painted schools and churches, beautified public spaces by cutting down weeds from neglected and overgrown lots, and done whatever else they could do. Their hard work and dedication toward rebuilding the city has proven contagious. Chapters of Youth Rebuilding New Orleans

have sprung up in other high schools around the city.

Hurricane Katrina devastated New Orleans and much of the Gulf Coast, but young people like the Stoudt brothers are working to build it back up.

Connect

American Red Cross
www.redcross.org
While it's been years since Hurricane Katrina, life is not yet back to normal on the Gulf Coast. Visit the Web site of the American Red Cross to see how you can help those in Louisiana, Mississippi, Alabama, and Texas affected by the hurricane.

Plant a community garden. Are you the kind of person who likes to get your hands dirty? If so, think about planting a community garden to help feed those who are hungry. Beyond producing food, a cooperative garden beautifies the community, promotes environmental sustainability, and brings people together in support of an important cause. You can take the following steps to reap a charitable harvest.

1. Work with community officials to plan a site and obtain the necessary permission. (You may also wish to check with officials at your school as to whether a garden might be planted there.)

2. Check with local aid agencies to determine what garden produce will help meet community needs.

3. Obtain all of the materials you'll need. You might fundraise (see page 15) to buy plants or solicit donations from local nurseries.

4. Plant your garden, involving people from all over the community. Assign participants specific tasks such as digging, planting, fertilizing, watering, harvesting, and delivering produce.

Take It Global

Join and support online communities addressing world poverty. Once, the only real way to connect with others was to write (via snail mail), call (on landlines), or meet up (in person). Today, the Internet and cell phones (which often double as cameras and computers) allow you to quickly and efficiently connect with important causes with a few clicks or keystrokes.

Organize a fundraiser to help reduce poverty. Many organizations are making important contributions to the fight against hunger and homelessness around the world. You might organize a fundraiser (see page 15) to help support this work.

When you've settled on a group you'd like to help (see the sidebar below for a few possibilities), you can stage your event. Be sure to emphasize to the public that proceeds will benefit the organization you've chosen. There are many fundraising events that you may consider:

- Perform a service. You might offer to clean up a local square or plaza, work in a neighbor's garden, or take care of others' pets in return for donations.

- Sell something. Many organizations have fundraisers in which foods,

coupons, or holiday gifts are sold in support of a worthy cause. You might follow this example and give the proceeds of your campaign to a local charity.

- Stage an event. You could organize a street carnival, an art fair, or a performance by an actor or theater group. Work with civic organizations, village or hamlet councils, and other community groups to establish a site location (such as the city gardens) and supporting participants (like food vendors).

Connect

Youth Against Poverty
www.youthagainstpoverty.org
Ryan Kitsu wanted to make others aware of the poverty experienced by people around the world. The problem was that nobody in his high school seemed interested in listening. So Ryan set up his own site about the topic. Youth Against Poverty now has tens of thousands of supporters online.

You Think!
www.youthink.worldbank.org
Read up on pressing issues at this Web site from the World Bank, a global institution that supports economic reconstruction efforts in the developing world. You can also comment on how you feel about debt relief, fair trade, and other topics.

Free the Children
www.freethechildren.com
Founded by youth hero Craig Kielburger (see pages 10–11), Free the Children is a Canada-based organization that supports children in need around the world. The group operates programs in over 45 countries, including initiatives to improve education, provide health care, and build water and sanitation systems.

DIFFERENCE MAKER

Mihiri Tillakaratne

Mihiri Tillakaratne lives in California, but part of her spirit resides in Sri Lanka. That's because her parents, immigrants from that Asian country, took her there many times as a child. As she grew older, Mihiri was startled by the poverty experienced by many in Sri Lanka's rural areas. She was also determined to help. Working with an aid organization from the country, Mihiri participated in a drive to fund preschool classes and to build a much-needed community bank. She also joined an effort to provide eyeglasses to those unable to afford them. This may seem like an odd combination of services, but they are exactly what the communities needed. Mihiri's priorities matched those of the people she was trying to help.

In December of 2004, a tsunami devastated many parts of southeast Asia, including much of Sri Lanka. Mihiri sprang into action, collecting donations from students in her high school for the relief effort. Then she traveled to other schools throughout California, collecting money, toys, and other goods she could send to support children in the affected region. And Mihiri didn't stop there. In a matter of months, she helped her temple raise $25,000 for relief efforts—enough money to build new homes for 50 families left homeless by the tsunami.

There seems no end to Mihiri's drive to help Sri Lankans. She's currently working on initiatives to provide rural areas with clean water, more education opportunities, technology centers, and a lot of other services the communities need. To learn more about Mihiri's efforts, visit www.empoweravillage.org.

Connect

NetAid
www.netaid.org
Mihiri's work on behalf of Sri Lankans has been recognized by multiple organizations, including NetAid—a network of high school students working to end global poverty. Visit the Web site to team up with other students and learn about volunteer and training opportunities. NetAid is closely associated with MercyCorps (www.mercycorps.org), another organization helping people in need.

Volunteer abroad. There are many opportunities to take your desire to help others out into the world. Organizations that provide international volunteer opportunities have programs that vary a great deal. It's important to research them to find the one that's best for you. Following are a few places to begin looking; others appear throughout this book.

Connect

International Cultural Youth Exchange
www.icye.org
This exchange organization offers service opportunities in over 30 countries. You might help educate children, participate in economic revitalization projects, or be involved in another available position. International Cultural Youth Exchange is a program partner of the European Voluntary Service, a European Commission initiative to promote active citizenship. Visit the Web site for a full listing of host nations and project information.

Kiwanis Key Club International
www.keyclub.org
Kiwanis Key Club International is a long-running program that gives teens opportunities to serve others. With a membership of nearly 250,000, this youth-led organization involves students in social action at both the local and global levels. Log on to the Web site to contact regional offices in Latin America, Europe, the United States, and Asia-Pacific.

Rotary International
www.rotary.org
Rotary International is an organization with members in more than 200 countries. The group works to provide humanitarian services in every part of the world, including through student exchanges. The program allows teens the opportunity to experience other cultures while at the same time filling volunteer needs in host communities. Visit the organization's Web site for details on exchange positions currently available.

DIFFERENCE MAKER

Nastassia Marina Bondarenko-Edwards

Walking through the dusty streets and scattered shops of Concordia, Brazil, 17-year-old Nastassia Marina Bondarenko-Edwards watched bareback children dart past her clothed in only ragged shorts. "I asked myself over and over, 'What can I do?'" Nastassia, on a Rotary Club International Exchange Program, was far from her home of Victoria, Australia.

Brazil has many beautiful places with strong economies, but Nastassia grew attached to one impoverished area of Concordia. She wanted to do something to help. Nastassia got her opportunity when she volunteered at an orphanage with over 320 children. She played soccer and jumped rope with the kids. On some visits she taught them about Australia and told them tales of things that had happened to her. They loved the games and stories from her life, and Nastassia and the children quickly developed close friendships.

Spending time with the kids at the orphanage was great, but Nastassia decided she wanted to do more. Children's Day—a Brazilian holiday on which young people are honored and receive gifts—was coming up. Nastassia knew, though, that the kids in the orphanage would receive nothing on the special day. That is, unless she did something about it. She emailed her Rotary members back in Australia asking for donations to support Children's Day and hoped for the best.

As the holiday approached, Nastassia was surprised by the amount of money that came from fellow Rotary members. Not only was she able to provide small gifts for the children on Children's Day, but she could buy new playground equipment and musical instruments. These things went beyond the celebration of a holiday. They were long-term improvements to the orphanage that the children could use for years.

At the end of her stay in Brazil, Nastassia reluctantly left the children she had come to know so well. She had become a big sister and provided them with much—but not nearly as much as they had given her in return.

Health and Safety

I believe if young people become more involved with solving global problems, this world will be a better place.

—Natsuno Shinagawa, 18, Global Activist

What Are the Facts?

Health and safety are basic human needs. Unfortunately, billions of people across the planet live in conditions that endanger their lives. Women and children are most often affected by these situations.

Disease, war, water shortages, famine, natural disasters, and unsanitary living conditions all contribute to millions of deaths each year.

People in wealthy countries or regions that are relatively peaceful also face health and safety risks, though not on the same

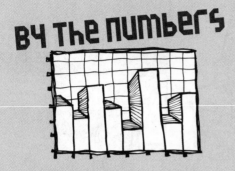

BY The numbers

Health and Safety:

➤ Worldwide, about 1.1 billion people do not have access to clean water. Approximately 2.6 billion have no access to proper sanitation. (UNICEF, www.unicef.org)

➤ About 1.8 billion children die each year around the world due to lack of clean water or sanitation services. (United Nations Development Programme, www.undp.org)

➤ Over 42 million people are infected with HIV/AIDS. Nearly three-quarters of all cases occur in sub-Saharan Africa. (World Health Organization, www.who.int)

➤ About 2 million people die each year from preventable diseases because they haven't received vaccinations. (World Health Organization, www.who.int)

➤ In the United States, nearly 1.4 million violent crimes are committed each year, including over 16,000 murders. (U.S. Department of Justice, www.usdoj.gov)

➤ An estimated 171 million children worldwide are exposed to dangerous work conditions that threaten their health. (UNICEF, www.unicef.org)

➤ Each day, about 166,000 students in the United States miss school because they don't feel safe there. (National Education Association, www.nea.org)

scale as in the developing world. This section offers ways you can improve the health and safety of others in your community and around the globe.

Keep It Local

Address bullying and violence in your school. Did you know that 10 to 15 percent of students in the United States report being bullied on a regular basis? Tragic school shootings make the news, but many other forms of abuse in schools go unreported. Here are some ways you can work to make your school a place where everyone feels safe and respected.

■ Stand up and speak out against bullying or teasing. Immediately report incidents to adults at your school. Reach out to those who are being put down or humiliated. Let your friends and others know that you have zero tolerance for disrespect or harm (physically or verbally) of others.

■ If your school doesn't have an anti-bullying program, talk with school staff about developing one. Work with teachers, administrators, counselors, and others to get everyone educated on the topic. If you encounter resistance, pursue the issue with the student council or another representative body.

- Organize an assembly on the responsible use of email, mobile phones, and instant messaging. Cyberbullying is increasingly being used to put down, exclude, and threaten others. These incidents include sharing personal or false information about someone on Web sites and sending pictures or videos meant to humiliate others. Help make people at your school aware that these actions are serious, hurtful, and unacceptable.

Promote public safety. When everyone in a town or neighborhood is alert and looking to help others, the whole community benefits. Here are some ways you can do your part.

- Become trained in first aid. Be sure you're able to respond with CPR (cardiopulmonary resuscitation) and other first-aid procedures. Many schools provide students with certification classes. If yours does not, you might find a class through Red Cross and Red Crescent organizations (www.ifrc.org).

Connect

International Safe Schools Committee
www.intlsafeschools.com
If you're interested in making your school a safer place, visit the site of this affiliate of the World Health Organization. You'll find information on peacemaking programs designed to unite students, teachers, and administrators. Discover how schools all over the globe are working toward seven critical goals of nonviolence and respect—and how yours can join.

Students Against Violence Everywhere (SAVE)
www.nationalsave.org
With groups in Iceland, Canada, and the United States, Students Against Violence Everywhere networks young people who are confronting bullying in schools and violence in communities. Find information online about conflict resolution, peacemaking workshops, and tools for starting a chapter of the group in your school. You'll be joining the effort to promote safety and respect among students.

- Familiarize yourself with any disaster plans that exist for where you live, work, and go to school. For example, would you know what to do if someone were to bring a weapon to class? Do you know the emergency plan for your city in the event of a natural disaster? Whatever the potential dangers, it's important to be prepared if and when something happens. Share information you learn with others.

- Do your part to address neighborhood crime. Stopping crime begins with vigilance. You might go a step further and unite others in support of a peaceful community. Get to know your neighbors and consider joining local police, community organizers, and citizens to form an anticrime partnership.

- Crime is not the only public-safety hazard a community faces. Raise awareness about any local health dangers—for example, the contamination of drinking water. Attend a council meeting to initiate dialogue with officials about solving the problem. If it becomes necessary, organize others in a demonstration to support your position. Document your efforts on a photo- or video-sharing site to help gather momentum for your cause.

Point & Click

World Health Organization (WHO)
www.who.int
The World Health Organization is the medical agency of the United Nations. Networking the resources of nearly 200 nations, the WHO serves as an authority on global health. Visit the Web site for information on epidemics of disease and other world health emergencies. You'll also find statistics, prevention information, and other helpful material you can use to promote health and safety.

Saul Alexander Torres

Sixteen-year-old Saul Alexander Torres watched people die in the streets from illness, car accidents, and other injuries in his native Nejapa, El Salvador. With no hospital in the municipality, people did not have access to the kind of health care that could save their lives. Saul knew that the nearest medical facility—90 kilometers away—was impossibly far. Even worse, Nejapa had no ambulance to transport people who were hurt or ill.

In 1992, Saul decided it was time for something to be done. While a municipal hospital did not seem possible, a team of first responders did. Saul became trained in first aid and began patrolling the streets of Nejapa, responding to accidents and other health crises. He also began teaching lifesaving skills to his friends and other teens—some as young as 12 years old—so that more citizens would be prepared to help in emergencies.

This was progress, but some illnesses and injuries needed medical attention that only a hospital could provide. "If only we had an ambulance, we could rush the wounded to the hospital. If only we had an old van." Saul was old enough to drive, but where could he and his crew get the funds to buy a vehicle?

Saul led the first responders to present their case before the local government. He explained that they did not have any means to transport people who needed treatment in a hospital. The Nejapa officials wanted to help—and while a brand new ambulance was not in their budget, the officials could help the first responders buy an old van.

Although it did not have a lot of the equipment you might find in an ambulance, the van was a huge help in saving lives. Some nights Saul and his crew would make four runs to the hospital, sleeping in the Nejapa community center, where they could remain on call. Over the course of five years, the group helped save the lives of more than 5,530 people—even treating gunshot wounds and delivering babies.

When Hurricane Mitch—one of the deadliest storms on record—struck El Salvador in the summer of 1998, Saul and his rescue crew were there. They were the principal coordinators of relief efforts in Nejapa, helping the injured and distributing food and clothing. Their only setback in saving lives occurred when the old van coughed, sputtered, and broke down for good. The crew quickly went door-to-door to collect money to buy another vehicle, so they could continue to help the sick and injured.

Promote teen health. In many developed nations, obesity and diabetes are at record levels among young people—a fact that experts blame largely on poor diets and lack of exercise. Other severe health problems can also affect teens, including sexually transmitted diseases and addiction. Knowledge is often the key to changing behavior. Play a role in making others aware of the potentially deadly effects of bad habits and destructive choices. Following are a few ways you can start.

- Participate in a school-wide campaign on an important health issue. You might propose an initiative to ban vending machines that sell soda and junk food or advocate for healthier menu options in the lunch program. Get the support of student groups, and involve any teachers and parents who are willing to back your cause. You might even make the campaign part of a health or nutrition class.

- Address risky behavior. Many of the most severe health and safety issues teens face—the result of sex, drug and alcohol abuse, or reckless driving—are

Child and Adolescent Health and Development
www.who.int/child-adolescent-health
This site from the World Health Organization has information on virtually every health issue young people face. Go online for information on nutrition, sexual health, and much more. With an international perspective, the site is a great source of information for any health campaigns you might take part in.

Students Against Destructive Decisions (SADD)
www.sadd.org
With hundreds of thousands of members across Canada, New Zealand, and the United States, this youth organization works to inform teens about the high risks of such behaviors as underage drinking, drug use, and impaired driving. You can visit the Web site to learn about youth trends and find out how to start a SADD chapter in your school.

100 percent preventable. Do your part to educate others about the effects of dangerous behaviors. Consider partnering with a local youth organization or medical facility on your initiative.

- Be a positive role model. Take care of yourself by eating healthful meals and staying active. Avoid actions that put you or others in harm's way. It sounds simple, but if people see you making positive choices, they are more likely to follow your example.

DIFFERENCE MAKER

Shannon Sullivan

Many young people don't know the best techniques for staying safe online. Shannon Sullivan, a sophomore from Wood-Ridge, New Jersey, wants to change that. Shannon helped found a chapter of Teenangels in her school. Based in the United States, Teenangels is an organization devoted to helping teenagers protect themselves online—from predators, privacy invasion, identity theft, and other dangers.

But Shannon's work doesn't stop with educating teens. She and other Teenangels advise technology corporations, including AOL, Microsoft, Disney, and Yahoo!, on safety issues from a teen perspective. In 2006, Shannon testified before the U.S. House of Representatives Department of Commerce—a group that helps regulate new media like the Internet. In her testimony, Shannon talked about the work of Teenangels. She emphasized that the group is not against social-networking sites, online gaming, or other Internet applications—teens enjoy many benefits from them—but is working to see that new technologies are overseen responsibly and safety campaigns receive funding. On this last issue, Shannon's testimony before the committee was something of a celebration. Teenangels had just been awarded a $50,000 funding measure by the U.S. Department of Justice to continue the important work.

While there will likely always be some risks online, the next generation of Internet users is likely to be quite tech-savvy and safe—especially as Shannon and Teenangels across the nation continue their safe-surfing campaign.

Connect

Teenangels
www.teenangels.org
If you'd like to follow Shannon's lead and get involved in this project, visit the Teenangels site. You might join an education program to inform others about Internet dangers, collaborate with law enforcement, or provide technical support.

Take It Global

Become a universal health-care advocate. Civil rights activist Dr. Martin Luther King Jr. once said, "Of all the forms of inequality, injustice in health care is the most shocking and inhumane." The fact is that the majority of the world's people do not have access to adequate health care. Many regions of the globe lack resources and modern health-care equipment. In wealthy nations, care is often available but so expensive that it is out of reach for many people. Following are ways you can help improve this situation.

- Advocate for health care as a basic, undeniable human right. To find out how you can act, visit the site of the People's Health Movement (www.phmovement.org), an organization overseeing the global Right to Health and Health Care Campaign. At the site you can contribute your name to an online petition, research health-care trends, and stay updated on current developments.

- Governments and large businesses most often play the biggest roles in delivering health care. In many places, however, community organizations are increasingly providing health services, whether it's for reproductive health or counseling. In many cases, these organizations fill needs overlooked by traditional health institutions—often in impoverished areas where people would otherwise go without care. To support this work, consider volunteering with a local agency. You might, for example, help in reception, database management, or fundraising efforts.

Connect

World Vision
www.worldvision.org
World Vision operates aid programs in some of the regions most affected by disease. Visit the Web site to learn how you can help end epidemics and support those (including orphaned children) left in their wake. Group opportunities are also available for faith communities.

Doctors Without Borders
www.doctorswithoutborders.org
This organization carries out humanitarian aid missions around the world—many in the fight against disease. Visit the site to learn more about how you can help bring equipment, medicine, and medical professionals to areas in need.

Provide services in the wake of a natural disaster. Earthquakes, hurricanes, tsunamis, and other disasters can affect a region for months and years. Damage to infrastructure can lead to widespread homelessness, disruptions in food and water supplies, and many other problems that put people's health and safety at risk. Get involved in helping people affected by disasters—whether it's collecting and donating supplies for those affected or traveling to a location where you can help on the ground.

Support an agency confronting a global health epidemic. Many organizations supply lifesaving treatments and medications to regions affected by epidemics. Efforts are under way to provide more vaccinations and to prevent further spread of illness through education initiatives. You might pitch in by raising money, generating awareness, or volunteering for one of the organizations working to eliminate disease and to protect people from unsanitary living conditions.

Connect

Global Youth Coalition on HIV/AIDS
www.youthaidscoalition.org
Linking over 3,500 youth HIV/AIDS activists, organizers, and peer-educators, this international organization works to inform young people about the epidemic and involve them as representatives at international conferences. At the Web site you'll learn about ways you can join this important cause.

International Federation of Red Cross and Red Crescent Societies (IFRC)
www.ifrc.org
The IFRC is the one-stop organization for disaster relief. Finding an opportunity near you is likely because the federation combines the relief efforts of 185 nations around the world. Formed nearly a century ago in response to the humanitarian needs that emerged after World War I, the IFRC helps those who are hurt, displaced, or otherwise in need. Included in their efforts are initiatives to provide immunizations against measles, polio, and other diseases.

United Methodist Committee on Relief (UMCOR)
www.umcor.org
UMCOR works to help people around the world who are affected by conflicts and natural disasters. You can help through one of the many volunteer positions, such as preparing emergency kits with vital supplies and sending them to areas of need. Visit the Web site for more information on this and other opportunities.

DIFFERENCE MAKER

Natsuno Shinagawa

Eighteen-year-old Natsuno Shinagawa is honest. She admits she didn't know a lot about AIDS at first. To her, it had always seemed far away—a disease that only affected other people. That was before Natsuno joined a 2005 UNICEF program near her home in Tochigi, Japan, a city just outside of Tokyo. In the program, Natsuno learned a lot about the epidemic, its devastating effects, and how people were helping bring it to an end. It wasn't long before she was an expert on the topic of AIDS and a strong advocate for those affected by it.

"In Japan," she said, "there are too many youth who are unaware of what's happening around the world." Natsuno wanted to help remedy that. In workshops, Natsuno explained to peers that the disease is not just the problem of a few select countries, but a global epidemic that affects everyone. She told of people dying by the millions, of orphaned children starving and with no access to school or other opportunities that might help improve their lives. The picture she painted was a terrible one, but it was important to make the crisis real to her audience.

Natsuno continues to bring attention to the AIDS epidemic as well as other issues confronting the world. She hopes to one day work for the United Nations and focus on development programs in Africa. According to Natsuno, solving global challenges should be a priority for all people, especially teens who bring a fresh perspective to situations. "I believe if young people become more involved with solving global problems, this world will be a better place."

Connect

UNICEF
www.unicef.org/aids
The AIDS epidemic is one focus of the Millennium Development Goals—efforts being undertaken to improve global health. UNICEF is a key organization in coordinating these efforts around the world. Visit the Web page about the AIDS epidemic to learn how you can contribute to this important cause.

Join a development project with an international organization. In the developing world, resources are often so scarce that many people's basic needs are not met. For example, one of six people on Earth does not have access to clean water. Two out of five do not have proper sanitation. The need for development projects around the world is huge. Consider getting involved in one of these efforts, perhaps with your family or a faith group. Following are some opportunities you might take to make a difference.

Global Volunteers
www.globalvolunteers.org
This organization involves volunteers in service all over the world—including water and sanitation services in developing nations, teaching and health-care opportunities, and construction projects. Visit the site to find a full listing of available positions and information on the application process.

United Planet
www.unitedplanet.org
A cultural exchange program with volunteers in over 150 countries, United Planet offers short-term (1–12 weeks) and long-term (6–12 months) volunteer positions. Groups (such as faith communities) can also apply for placement. Visit the Web site to search opportunities by duration, region, and area of focus.

Canada World Youth
www.cwy-jcm.org
This organization places Canadian youth in community-building positions around the country and the world. Canada World Youth features opportunities of varying length and intensity—from short-term construction projects to long-term tutoring opportunities. You can find more information at the Web site.

DIFFERENCE MAKER

Saroj Rawat

Lights, camera, action! The camera operator began to record, capturing panoramic shots of . . . trash. It was 2003, and a film crew was shooting footage of a Delhi, India, garbage dump. It looked like pretty much any other landfill, except for one startling thing: Young children were climbing among the heaps of smelly trash. To help their families get money to buy food, the children were forced to pick through the piles for objects they could sell. Amidst the junk were syringes, broken glass, and other dangerous items.

Saroj Rawat, 15, was part of the film crew working on the movie. It was a documentary being made with support from Plan International, a non-governmental organization with health projects in over 50 countries. The crew's goal was to make children aware of the dangers of the dump, and to convince them that spending time there was taking away from a much better opportunity for future success—an education.

When the film was complete, Saroj and her group screened it in the neighborhood, and the community came out to view what the crew had been working on. At the viewing, parents and children alike learned about the risk of injury, infection, and disease that exist at the landfill. Seeing these dangers captured on film made a big impact on the audience. Many

families kept their children from returning to the dump, and instead, sent them to the local school.

This isn't the only movie on Saroj's résumé. She and the rest of the crew tackled many other issues including tobacco addiction. The group released a documentary titled *Addicted Innocence*, which examined tobacco's negative health effects and aimed to persuade youth to avoid the habit. With this and other vital health information to share, the group had found an effective way to get the message out—movies. The group won many awards for their work.

But Saroj is a young woman of many talents, including public speaking. She was one of the main speakers at a 2003 New Delhi conference on sexual abuse in developing nations. She told tragic stories about girls and young women who were victims of date rape and other forms of abuse and explained that Indian culture sometimes allowed these crimes to be

covered up. Families often refused to go to the police because they wanted to protect family honor. Saroj emphasized the importance of families acknowledging abuse and supporting victims so that cases could be pursued. If not, abuse would continue.

As she has worked to change people's minds on vital health and safety concerns, Saroj has not lost her belief in a better world. And she thinks youth are an important factor in effecting change: "It feels good to know that as children we have rights, and when we speak, people are forced to sit up and listen."

Connect

Plan International
www.plan-international.org
Saroj was an advocate with Plan International—an organization that works with children, families, and communities to create positive social change. Plan has programs in support of children's rights, education opportunities, health, and economic sustainability. Log on to the Web site to learn more.

Education

 I strongly feel that educating the children of today is an investment in a happy and safe future of the world.
—Ram Gopalakrishnan, 16, Global Activist

What Are the Facts?

Education has been called the greatest equalizer. It gives people of all backgrounds the opportunity to make their lives better. Unfortunately, many around the world are not able to attend school or advance their learning because of economic hardships. Children and young adults may feel forced to work to help support their families. A lack of adequate education resources in many developing regions can add to this challenge.

Education is crucial for improving living conditions across the planet. In areas with political corruption and cultural conflicts, denial of education is one of the ways

By The numbers

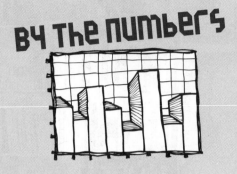

Education:

➤ Nearly one billion people are illiterate. The great majority of these people live in the developing world. About two-thirds are women. (United Nations Development Programme, www.undp.org)

➤ About 134 million school-age children across the globe have never been to school. Most of these young people are girls. (CARE, www.care.org)

➤ Education opportunities are most limited in rural areas. One out of three children of primary age in rural regions of the developing world is not enrolled in school. (UNESCO, www.unesco.org)

➤ Over 10 percent of students in the United States quit school before high school graduation. (United States Department of Education, www.ed.gov)

that ruling groups try to maintain power. Those who are uneducated are less able to defend themselves against injustices. It's also difficult for them to join the economic and power structures. Women, minorities, and people living in poverty are those most severely affected.

People who are uneducated often have no way to escape poverty, and many of their basic health and nutrition needs can go unmet. Schools, especially in developing nations, also serve as places where people learn about epidemics affecting a society. People who are not educated on these issues are more likely to act in ways that can make a situation worse (for example, by further spreading disease). This section has suggestions to help in the effort to expand education opportunities.

Keep It Local

Tutor others at your school. Many opportunities exist to help others learn. Some schools have programs in which secondary students work with primary grade children—often as part of a service project. You might also work with peers who have disabilities or challenges that may make learning difficult. Depending on your personal strengths and interests, you could volunteer to help others with reading, writing, math, or another subject. Look into programs your school has in place, or, if there are none, ask a teacher or counselor to help you start one.

DIFFERENCE MAKER

Ram Gopalakrishnan

"How does a ninth grader who is 16 years old open a school?" Ram Gopalakrishnan asked himself. Ram knew that his community in Noida, India, needed a place where young people could go to learn. Many of the people were poor, had little education, and could not read. In fact, about half of all Indians were illiterate.

Ram knew he could not personally teach half a billion people, but he did believe he could make a difference locally. Inspired by the Millennium Development Goal of providing education for all people, Ram decided he'd try to open a school of his own. This was a big challenge for an ordinary 16-year-old without a lot of rupees to spend. So in 2000, Ram began soliciting donations from family members, neighbors, teachers, and pretty much everyone else he knew for his Eradication of Illiteracy Project.

Ram was eventually able to buy enough supplies, including books, paper, pencils, and erasers, to support a small classroom of children. But that brought up another dilemma. Ram didn't really have a classroom (or any room) where kids could study. After quite a lot of asking around the neighborhood, Ram at last lined up some free space in a local garage. With some work, Ram was able to convert the space into a decent classroom. Searching for instructors was tough, but Ram eventually found two teachers willing to volunteer at the school.

When Ram opened the doors of his school, the faint smell of gasoline and oil still hung in the air, and only three kids showed up. But the enthusiasm of these students began to entice other neighborhood youth to join. It wasn't long before attendance at the garage school swelled to 30 students, each child studying language, math, art, and other subjects. These were all young people—mostly girls—who might not otherwise have had the chance to attend school.

When Ram went to college in Singapore in 2006, he left the little garage school to his capable younger brother, Raj, who shares his passion of educating others. "For all the difficulties faced by us," Ram says, "we have been rewarded in a beautiful way, which will inspire many others to make our world a better place to live in."

Support education initiatives. Funding education is one of the most important investments a society can make in its people. It's essential to stay current on efforts in your community to ensure that young people are not being shortchanged when it comes to learning. Following are some ways you can be an education advocate.

- Voice your views in a letter to the editor of your local newspaper. Discuss in your letter funding targets you'd like to see schools receive. You might also take a look at operating expenses (which are often a matter of public record) and write about how diminished funding will hurt area schools.

- Campaign for or against specific education policies. Learn about pending initiatives and contact officials to comment on them. You might set up a Web site to explore the pros and cons of policy. Also consider petitioning others online (www.ipetition.com) or in your neighborhood.

- Join education organizations and associations. Look into becoming a member of a regional or national group supporting education. Many of these organizations send email alerts and action suggestions when critical initiatives are being considered.

- Organize a group of students to present your views at an open meeting of the school board or a legislative body debating education issues. Work to get on the meeting's agenda and present your perspectives on student issues. To increase the visibility of your group, consider inviting members of the media to cover the event.

DIFFERENCE MAKER

Darko Lovric

What would you do if your school were boring—really, really boring? No extra-curricular activities—no sports or drama or anything else. The teachers didn't care and the other students, well, they didn't really care either. Darko Lovric saw this in his high school in Zagreb, Croatia. But instead of tuning out, he decided to make things happen.

In 2001, Darko founded Pokret (which means "movement"), an initiative devoted to improving his school. His objective for the program was to make the school day more relevant to teens' lives and get the students to care about their education. Pokret paired up students with young professionals from the community who served as mentors. Pokret provided a way for teens to develop new skills and get real-world experience. Finally challenged in ways they could relate to, the students began to study with genuine interest.

Darko's influence on education did not end there. He developed a Pokret curriculum with Horizont, a non-governmental organization instituting education programs throughout Croatia. The curriculum focused on instruction in economics, communications, and other subjects that interested students and would help them succeed after high school. The program was so popular and successful that it was soon implemented by Croatia's Ministry of Education in eight other high schools.

Darko Lovric, with his movement called Pokret, has helped improve the state of education for his peers. Maybe more important, he has inspired them to imagine a brighter future—one in which they have control. After all, rather than sit back and accept what was handed to him, Darko stood up—for the education, the opportunity, and the life that he and other Croats deserve.

DIFFERENCE MAKER

Jacob Komar

Jacob Komar recognized that many people don't own computers or even live near a place where they can use one. Even in a wealthy nation like the United States, a huge digital divide separates those who have access to technology and those who don't.

In 2002, Jacob saw an opportunity to help narrow this divide. He learned that a local school planned to throw away 30 computers, and he acted quickly to save the machines from the landfill. The computers were older models, and some needed a little work. But this wasn't really a problem for Jacob, who—even at age nine—

happened to be a computer genius. When he was done making technical tweaks and updating software, Jacob worked to distribute the machines in his home city of Burlington, Connecticut, with the help of a social-service agency devoted to helping people in need.

What began as an effort to recycle 30 computers grew into Computers for Communities, an organization Jacob founded to continue his work of bringing machines to people in need. Five years on, Jacob is now 14, and his organization has grown with him. He has refurbished over 1,000 computers and placed them with families who might not otherwise been able to afford them. Computers for Communities now also provides tech training for those who need it.

Says Jacob, "Our goal is to bring all of the people who don't have tech skills into the category of those who do have skills." Computers for Communities is steadily helping make this happen.

Connect

Computers for Communities
www.computers4communities.org
Log on to the Web site of Jacob's organization to see how you can get involved in the effort to connect others. Find information on starting a program in your area, joining an existing group, mentoring others, or making a donation.

Teach others in a community education program. Many community agencies, libraries, and houses of worship offer classes and activities to help people build academic and life skills. These can vary a great deal by area. If you live in a place significantly affected by immigration, for example, literacy courses might be in high demand. There might be a strong need for career-development classes that teach people about job applications and interviews. Computer courses are also often available. Find a program near you that complements your interests and skills.

Take It Global

Organize a book drive. There are many places where books are in short supply. Setting up a book drive is a fun way to help fill a need and unite people for a good cause. Here are steps for setting up an event:

1. Arrange for drop-off locations, including area schools, places of worship, and government buildings. Create a container with a distinctive look so that people know where to donate books.

2. Publicize your event. Get the word out to other students at your school. Contact features editors at newspaper, TV, radio, or Web news outlets and ask them to profile the project. Be sure to provide a full list of book drop-off locations, hours, and the dates of your drive.

3. Tie the book drive to other local happenings. For example, the drive's final event might coincide with a reading by a local author or a concert.

4. Collect gently used books from libraries, schools, bookstores, and publishers. You might also arrange a deal with local stores to provide discounts or gifts for those bringing in donations.

Connect

Bridge to Asia
www.bridge.org
Did you know that books can be extremely expensive in many parts of Asia? In China, the price of one medical textbook can equal the monthly salary of a doctor. To make books more available to students, Bridge to Asia collects books and donates them to over 1,000 Asian universities. Log on to the Web site to learn more about how you can help.

Books for Africa
www.booksforafrica.org
There is an urgent need for books in many parts of Africa. Since 1988, Books for Africa has donated over 15 million books to more than 20 countries. The group's Web site offers details on how you can become involved in the effort to promote literacy and learning.

Fundraise to buy supplies for schools.
Books are not the only education items
needed in developing nations. Often there
are shortages of paper, pens, pencils, fold-
ers, and other basic supplies, not to mention limited resources for desks, training,
and teacher salaries. Consider setting up a
campaign to collect basic supplies, using a
similar approach to that of a book drive. Or
you might organize an event to raise funds
for one of the organizations supporting
global education initiatives.

Point & Click

**United Nations
Cyberschoolbus**
www.cyberschoolbus.un.org
You'll find information at this site
on international education initiatives
under way in support of the
Millennium Development Goals.
Take the opportunity to participate
in the online education community—
which includes other people
in your school. There are many
classroom projects to help find
solutions to global problems.
Projects deal with war, poverty,
human rights, and other important
issues.

Connect

UNICEF
www.unicef.org
Visit the UNICEF site to learn how you can support the education of young
people around the world. The organization, which is part of the United Nations,
supports many learning initiatives in the developing world, including the "School
in a Box"—an all-in-one set of supplies for teachers in regions affected by disasters or extreme poverty.

Free the Children
www.freethechildren.org
Based in Canada, Free the Children sponsors many campaigns, including education programs in developing nations. Log on to the Web site to learn how you
can help build schools and provide education supplies in nations across the globe.

DIFFERENCE MAKER

Zuhra Bahman

Zuhra Bahman was 16 when violence forced her family to leave their native Afghanistan in 1999. The family settled first in Pakistan and then in England. Though Zuhra was away, her home nation was always on her mind—she spoke about it every chance she got. She talked to groups about the Afghanistan she had been forced to leave. She told of the horrors of the Taliban regime that held power, including the severe oppression of women.

It was important to Zuhra to raise awareness about the challenges Afghan people faced. But her longtime goal was to create more education opportunities in her country, especially for girls who had been denied the right to go to school. When Zuhra left Afghanistan, she was the only girl in her village who knew how to read. She believed girls, with an education, could be more involved in community and government matters and have more influence in how their families lived. But progress under the Taliban regime seemed impossible.

Zuhra's opportunity came after the United States began a military campaign to remove the Taliban from power in 2002. Though dangerous, Zuhra—with the help of UNICEF and the Afghan Ministry of Education—was able to make headway on her goal. She helped build a library in a girls' high school in Kabul, the nation's capital.

Zuhra has continued her work through the Afghan Youth Fund, an organization devoted to education initiatives in her native country. With the organization's help, a second library at another girls' high school has been built, and plans are under way for a third. Two education centers for young people in need have also been opened. At these centers, teens receive nutritious meals and learn real-world skills they can use to improve their lives. The Afghan people still face some difficult challenges, but as Zuhra says, "Education is the solution to many problems."

Connect

Afghan Youth Fund
www.afghanyouthfund.org
Visit the site of Zuhra's organization to learn how you can support youth in Afghanistan. You'll find information on education and health initiatives taking place in Kabul and surrounding areas, and you'll get ideas for what you can do to help.

One World Youth Project
www.oneworldyouthproject.org
One World Youth Project is a program that connects secondary schools around the globe. Schools work together on United Nations Millennium Development Goals, with each school implementing a collaborative service project.

People to People International
www.ptpi.org
This organization works to connect youth everywhere. With options for all ages, the programs are designed to promote greater understanding among cultures. Students communicate over the course of a school year while working on mutual projects. Service toward others is also a key element of the program.

U.N. Online Volunteering Service
www.onlinevolunteering.org
This site from the United Nations is a clearinghouse of online volunteer opportunities. Visit it to learn about causes to which you can contribute your talents as a translator, designer, or Web developer.

ServiceLeader.org
www.serviceleader.org
Visit this Web site for virtual volunteering opportunities. Some needs include grant researcher, database manager, proofreader, graphic designer, member services supporter, and many more.

Link with a school in another nation. Exchanging cultural information with people from other countries and regions can be an exciting way to learn new things and build understanding. Many programs enable classes to have this experience without leaving their schools (using the Internet or satellite communication). Students can share concerns and collaborate on potential solutions to global problems. Joint-service projects are often part of the curriculum. If this interests you, you might research programs and discuss options with your teacher and classmates.

Volunteer online. You can make a global difference without traveling. Online you might, for example, tutor a student in another country. Or you could serve as a translator. Many organizations are looking to present information in multiple languages. If you are fluent in at least two languages, you're an ideal candidate. You might also help a group build a Web site, raise funds, or complete any number of other online tasks.

Volunteer to teach others abroad. Volunteer positions for educating others can vary a great deal. You might teach your native language in another country. (If you're bilingual, great, but often you don't have to be.) There are also many opportunities to teach about computers, life skills, and other subjects. You can get started by reviewing program options.

Council on Standards for International Educational Travel (CSIET)
www.csiet.org
This nonprofit organization rates programs offering youth exchange. Visit the site for a listing of age requirements, cost estimates, financial aid information, and contact information for some of the most reputable programs.

Jewish Coalition for Service
www.jewishservice.org
Are you interested in working as a volunteer in another country? The Jewish Coalition for Service provides teaching opportunities abroad as well as the chance to participate in humanitarian efforts. Visit the Web site to learn more about available positions.

Rotary International
www.rotary.org
Rotary International supports many global education initiatives, including literacy programs for girls and women. You might also join community-building projects in the developing world. Visit the Web site or check with your local chapter for more information on opportunities.

DIFFERENCE MAKER

Ruth Bowling

School is often taken for granted by students in wealthy nations—so much so that many students drop out. But other teens, especially in parts of the developing world, have little or no access to education opportunities. In some regions, primary programs are scarce and there are virtually no secondary schools.

Ruth Bowling discovered this on her first day in the village of Abrafo in Ghana. Ruth was on a gap-year exchange before starting courses at a university in her native England. She was in Ghana to teach a class of young children, but worried whether she was truly ready. The children in her group didn't speak much English, and she wondered how she would communicate. A fortunate thing occurred when she discovered a way to reach the children through the universal language of play. These were young children, after all. A game of soccer got everyone excited and working together. When everyone was familiar with one another, the real work began.

Over three months, Ruth worked hard to help her class make progress. She also developed a strong connection with her students, who began to call her "Madam Ruth." During Ruth's time in Ghana, the students learned many new skills. When Ruth arrived, some kids hadn't known how to hold a pencil. Now the entire group was memorizing and writing the alphabet—just the way young children in a wealthy nation have the opportunity to do. Ruth proudly says, "The children were so bright and picked up ideas quickly." No doubt, "Madam Ruth" had something to do with that.

Environment and Conservation

" We have the power to change the world and to make it into a better place. "*
—Janine Licare, 13, Global Activist

What Are the Facts?

Our environment affects every aspect of life on Earth—including the air we breathe, the water we drink, and the food we eat. You might think environmental protection would top all other priorities. Unfortunately, conservation efforts are often made secondary to other pressures like economic development. For example, a government or company might decide that building up industry is more important than maintaining air and water quality or protecting other natural resources.

Culture can also influence how effectively people address environmental concerns. Many people are not educated about the impact their actions can have on the planet—or they may be aware of problems but avoid changing their behavior. Life in the United States, for instance, is heavily dependent on automobiles—despite diminishing energy sources and widespread belief that vehicle emissions are damaging the Earth's atmosphere. For some, driving is a matter of necessity to reach work or school. For others with access to mass-transit options, driving is often still favored for its convenience.

When it comes to protecting the environment, the challenge isn't that some people are against conservation, but that they are unwilling or unable to make more Earth-friendly choices. This section offers ideas for greener living and suggestions for promoting environmentalism in others.

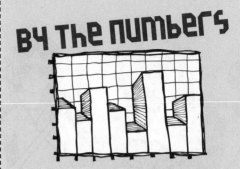

By The Numbers

Environment and Conservation:

➤ Deforestation is a major problem in nearly every region of the world. In Canada, an acre of ancient rain forest is cut down every 12 seconds. In Brazil, an acre is lost every nine seconds. (The Nature Conservancy, www.nature.org)

➤ The average person in the United States produces about 1,600 pounds of garbage each year. (United States Department of Energy, www.doe.gov)

➤ If current rates of human consumption and land use continue, it is expected that half of the planet's wildlife species will become extinct in the next 75 years. (Greenpeace, www.greenpeace.org)

➤ Drivers in the United States use over 385 million gallons of gasoline each day. (United States Department of Energy, www.doe.gov)

Keep It Local

Examine your habits. When talking about environmental issues, it's easy to blame big companies for eating up resources or polluting habitats. It can be harder to accurately gauge the effect our individual actions have on the planet. Do you drive or get a ride to places you might easily bike, bus, or walk to? Do you live in an energy-efficient home? Does your family recycle glass, aluminum, plastic, paper, and other reusable materials? The point is that many of the toughest environmental challenges could be reduced if more individuals made green living a priority for themselves. You can start by taking a close look at your lifestyle choices.

Celebrate Earth Day. Earth Day is celebrated in some parts of the world in March and in others on April 22. Regardless of when you mark the occasion, be sure to do something to help the planet on its special day. You might join a demonstration in support of an endangered species, pick up litter in a local park, or take part in a tree-planting event. And remember to make every day Earth Day.

Connect

Ecological Footprint Quiz
www.myfootprint.org
Would you like to figure out your impact on the environment? Log on to this Web site to discover how your habits affect the planet. The site features a program that determines your ecological "footprint" based on a short list of questions and the region of the world where you live. You can learn how your eco-friendliness stacks up against that of the average person and find resources promoting sustainable living.

Greener Choices
www.greenerchoices.org
People can make a big environmental difference based on the products they choose to buy (or not buy). For example, did you know that buying locally grown food can result in less environmental destruction? When you buy locally, you help reduce environmental costs associated with transporting food. The Greener Choices Web site offers more of these suggestions and Consumer Reports information on all kinds of eco-friendly products—from food to electronics.

Connect

Earth Day Network
www.earthday.net
The Earth Day Network was created by the organizers of the original Earth Day, which took place in 1970. Today the group connects environmental activists and coordinates eco-projects involving over half a billion people annually. Log on to the Web site to learn how you and your school can participate in events.

Greenpeace
www.greenpeace.org
Founded in 1971, Greenpeace is one of the oldest environmental protection organizations. The group serves as an advocate for many environmental causes, including preservation of the world's forests and oceans. Visit the Web site to find many ideas for taking action on important initiatives.

Organize a campaign to promote recycling. Many cities and towns have recycling programs of some kind, but separating plastic, glass, aluminum, paper, and other recyclable materials is often not required. People who do not understand how to recycle (or don't want to make an effort) often choose not to participate. Do your part to raise awareness about the positive effects recycling can have on your community and the planet at large. Don't forget to include information about the proper disposal of batteries, cell phones, and other techno-trash.

- Check in with local officials for information on recycling drop-off spots in your community. Often, these can be found outside of large markets, near a village square, or outside of public buildings. If there are currently no drop locations in your area, work with your town, district, or city council to establish some. Also collaborate with leaders to ensure there are adequate containers for recyclables and that they are picked up at regular intervals.

- Publicize your campaign. Share information on drop-off locations with the public. Involve others at your school and distribute flyers that detail the benefits of recycling. Post notices in public areas, such as a community center or post office. Also contact local media and seek ad space (in newspapers or on Web sites) to bring attention to the recycling program.

DIFFERENCE MAKER

Gabriella McCall

What would you do if all the birds in your neighborhood seemed to be disappearing? Gabriella McCall, a high school senior who happened to really like birds, began to worry this was happening in her community of Humacau, Puerto Rico. She also noticed that there was a lot of development going on in the neighborhood—malls, movie theaters, and houses were springing up all over the place. Gabriella wondered if there might be a connection and decided to investigate.

Gabriella knew it would be important to understand just what kinds of birds (and how many) were living in the neighborhood. Gabriella meticulously observed and recorded the species in the area. She took photos and notes on the bird populations. When she had completed her report, it was time to go public.

Gabriella organized an exhibition to share the information she had collected. She emphasized not only the importance of the birds' survival, but also what their declining numbers

might mean to everyone who lived in the area. A reduction in bird populations suggested an upset in the local ecosystem, an imbalance that could ultimately affect all living things in the area, including humans. She knew that the health and safety of people is dependent upon an environment that supports diverse species. Gabriella talked about the importance of responsible city planning to ensure that all life—bird, human, and otherwise—flourishes.

Gabriella's presentations were a huge success with children. Probably drawn in by Gabriella's slide show of colorful species and a conservation-minded computer game she created, the elementary students fell in love with all things feathered. Gabriella knew the importance of reaching young people; the very children before her would one day be making decisions about development in the region. As she brought her case for responsible development to the greater public, she knew a whole generation of birders was waiting in the wings to support her efforts.

Help maintain a local woodland or wetland. Environmental degradation happens, to some extent, virtually everywhere. You might know of a polluted pond or vanishing forestland near your home. It's important to get involved in environmental causes at the local level. After all, it's your (and your neighbors') health and quality of life at stake. What can you do?

- Monitor the health of a local body of water. Are any chemicals, heavy metals, or other contaminates present that could harm fish or wildlife? Have any nonnative species invaded and displaced plant or animal species? Some schools have incorporated analyzing local lakes and rivers into science classes. If your school has not, you might propose the idea to a teacher. Also consider involving local or regional environmental officials in your project.

- Work to save forestland. In some areas, logging companies are allowed to clear-cut forests so that not a single tree is left standing for many acres. Trees are also susceptible to disease—parasitic bugs can swoop in and destroy a forest in a matter of a few short years. Campaign against these or any other threats to forests in your area—whether it's by advocating for responsible logging or working with officials to stem the progression of disease.

- Get involved in the care of a local park. If you don't live near a lot of natural areas, make a difference by helping out in a city or borough park. There are many volunteer tasks you can perform to help green up urban areas—including planting trees and gardens, removing litter, or maintaining lawns. Contact your parks council for opportunities.

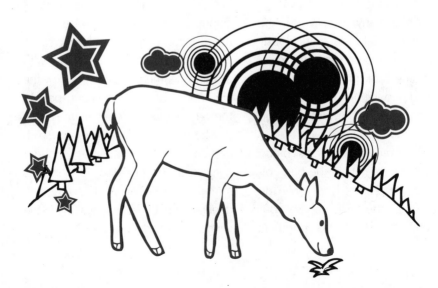

DIFFERENCE MAKER

Ben Banwart

Have you ever been riding in a car along a highway and seen one of those signs saying such-and-such group has adopted the next mile or kilometer of road for cleanup? Probably so. Maybe you've walked around with a bag picking up trash. To get an idea of Ben Banwart's contribution, take this idea and multiply it by about a thousand.

In 2000, Ben became the official Adopt-a-Park sponsor of Jackson Park, an 87-acre recreation area near his home in Shakopee, Minnesota. Because 87 acres is a lot of ground for one person to cover, Ben had to find a crew that cared about maintaining the park as much as he did. Ben found just the right people for the job when he asked the other guys in his Boy Scout troop to join him.

Rather than just picking up some litter and going home, however, Ben and his group undertook an entire ecological renovation project. They removed poisoned and damaged trees so that the remainder of the forest would not be affected by disease and cleared acres of buckthorn, a pest plant not native to the region. They planted hundreds of trees to secure slopes and provide more homes for area wildlife. Oh, and they also picked up a bunch of litter. Over the course of four years—a forest is never saved in a single day—Ben oversaw the complete redevelopment and renewal of Jackson Park.

The result? A beautiful, sustainable ecosystem where the public can gain a greater appreciation of the natural world.

Connect

World Organization of the Scout Movement
www.scout.org
Ben enlisted the help of his fellow Scouts to transform Jackson Park. Scouting provides many excellent opportunities to make a difference in communities all over the globe. Visit the Web site of the World Organization of the Scout Movement to find a group near you.

Take It Global

Support online environmental initiatives. Would you believe you can make a global environmental impact with a couple of mouse clicks? It's true. There are a number of sites where you can go to support efforts to save the planet. These sites have sponsors that contribute money to a cause based on how many people visit. Other Web sites can connect you with pro-planet petitions, policy alerts, and tools you can use to make a difference at the local level.

Distribute information to help others go green. One of the biggest obstacles people have in making environmentally friendly choices is a lack of information. Think about how you might inform others about green issues. If you like magazines, you might publish one on environmentalism. Maybe you're involved in a school or community group that addresses current affairs. If so, make environmentalism a front-and-center issue. Or perhaps you feel most comfortable airing your views online. Set up a Web site with information people can use to help the environment. Keep readers up to date with message boards, e-newsletters, and other Web applications. Following are a few topics to share information about.

Connect

The Rainforest Site
www.therainforestsite.com
Protect 11.4 square feet of endangered rain forest with one click—that's what this site enables you to do. Bookmark the site if you'd like to make a difference on a daily basis. You're allowed to participate one time every 24-hour period. To date, the site has sponsored the survival of hundreds of thousands of acres of forestland.

World Wildlife Fund
www.worldwildlife.org
Perhaps you've seen the World Wildlife Fund's iconic logo of a panda bear. In fact, the organization funds the protection of not just the panda bear but all kinds of species around the world. Visit the site to learn how you can help support the group's efforts to preserve the habitat and livelihood of endangered animals.

- Green housing. Spread the word about green housing—homes that incorporate recycled building materials and are energy efficient. Some homes also have rooftop gardens to minimize damaging runoff. Go to Global Green (www.globalgreen.org) to learn more about earth-friendly buildings and green cities.

- Energy efficiency and water use. Many people don't realize the impact their everyday energy and water habits have on the environment. Encourage people to winterize homes, limit use of air conditioning, and install low-flow showerheads. You can find other ideas at Campaign Earth (www.campaignearth.org).

- Toxic waste. Did you know that toxic waste is traded between countries? It's true. Wealthy nations—not wanting hazardous materials on their land—dump waste on developing countries in return for economic incentives. To learn more, visit the Web site of the Basel Action Network (www.ban.org) for more information.

- Transportation. In some parts of the world, the majority of people commute to and from school or work by car, often without seriously considering mass-transit options. Start a campaign about the positive environmental impact of mass transit, carpooling, and walking or biking to work or school.

DIFFERENCE MAKER

Janine Licare

When most people think of a rain forest, they picture tall green trees, lush groundcover, and animals scurrying everywhere. They don't usually imagine dusty roads, trucks rumbling around, and bulldozers belching out clouds of black smoke. Yet that's exactly what many parts of the rain forest look like—machines felling trees and plowing under native vegetation.

Connect

Kids Saving the Rainforest (KSTR)
www.kidssavingtherainforest.org
Scientists think there are hundreds of thousands of unknown species in Earth's rain forests. These are plants and animals that could offer clues about our world and insight into curing disease—not to mention that they're just really interesting to look at and study. Log on to the Web site of Kids Saving the Rainforest to learn how you can help in the effort to preserve habitats. You'll also find updates on what Janine is doing now in her effort to save forests.

No one had to tell Janine Licare about this desperate situation in the rain forest near her home in Manuel Antonio, Costa Rica. She witnessed it firsthand every day. Janine had seen forestland clear-cut. She'd seen countless animals crushed under the wheels of lumbering trucks. And, at nine years old, she decided she'd seen enough.

In 1999, Janine cofounded Kids Saving the Rainforest, an organization dedicated to preserving the forests and their wildlife. The group started out by mobilizing the community to help protect the titis—a species of monkeys being crushed by vehicles in huge numbers. With the clearing of the forests, the titis were not able to get around without crossing roads. Some tried to cross by climbing across power lines and were electrocuted. To help stop this, Kids Saving the Rainforest raised funds and built monkey bridges—ropes high above deadly roads where titis could move throughout the forest safely.

Janine, now 17, has continued to devote her energy to the forest

and its wildlife in other ways. Kids Saving the Rainforest has planted, to date, over 5,000 trees to help offset the destruction cause by logging. The organization has also opened an animal-rehabilitation center where it helps wounded animals and reintroduces them into the wild. Another important focus of the group is educating others about the rain forest and how to help save it. For this reason, Kids Saving the Rainforest has grown beyond the Costa Rican borders. Chapters of the organization have been formed all over the world, including in India, France, the United States, and many other areas.

Many people care about preserving rain forests. Janine developed a passion for it. More, she has a gift for inspiring the same feeling in others so that now a global brigade of eco-friends is working to save them. Because, as she says, "We have the power to change the world and to make it into a better place."

Investigate climate change. A consensus in the scientific community tells us that climate change is one of the most severe and pressing problems our planet faces. While the reasons behind the warming of the planet are still being fully explored, we know that reductions in carbon emissions and other human interventions can help improve the situation. Climate change is something that affects us all, and we all need to do our part to help reduce it. Join in the efforts of one of the many organizations addressing the problem.

Clean Air World
www.cleanairworld.org
This Web site features updates on what countries are doing (and not doing) to clean up air pollution. Included on the site is contact information for government agencies that oversee air quality. Log on to find out where you can direct your concerns about climate.

Fight Global Warming
www.fightglobalwarming.com
Visit this Web site from Environmental Defense, a conservation organization, to learn more about global warming. You'll find tools to figure out your impact, action tips you can use to help reduce harmful emissions, and opportunities to support political and economic policy that is environmentally responsible.

DIFFERENCE MAKER

Hao Yan

When Hao Yan, 18, learned about Roots and Shoots, an organization mobilizing youth in conservation and sustainable living efforts, he wanted to get involved. But there was a problem: No chapter of the environmental organization existed in his home city of Shanghai, China. So, Hao decided to form one.

Hao began recruiting other Chinese teens from his school. Things went a little slowly at first. At one point the group had only 10 members. That didn't stop them from fundraising and increasing public awareness about their mission. As word got out about Hao's chapter of Roots and Shoots, more and more people signed on to help. Soon they were in the midst of large projects preserving plant diversity on their school campus, organizing Earth Day celebrations, and instituting a school-wide recycling program.

An important part of the Roots and Shoots message is cultivating environmentalism in others. This also became an important focus for Hao's group. Many people in rural areas of China did not know a lot about sustainable living practices. To address this, the group began an outreach program that shared information on green living with people in some of these rural regions of the nation. Says Hao, "It's inspiring for youth activists to believe in the future of today's China and a society based on the active social involvement of the public."

Connect

Roots and Shoots
www.rootsandshoots.org
Hao decided to make his difference by forming a Roots and Shoots group. He's not alone—there are over 8,000 chapters of the organization in nearly 100 countries. Log on to the Web site to learn more about naturalist Jane Goodall, founder of the group, and how you can get involved in conservation efforts.

Volunteer around the world to help out on environmental projects. It's becoming more and more common for people to take "volunteer vacations"—trips to other countries on which they do something for local environments. There are many opportunities to be an eco-tourist by doing something for Mother Earth. Trips can differ a great deal in terms of qualifications, region, and length. Make sure to do your homework on programs before buying a plane ticket or making other travel plans.

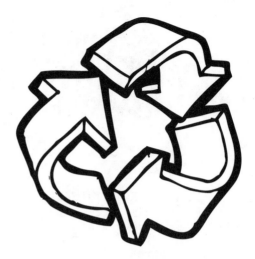

Connect

Council on Standards for International Educational Travel (CSIET)
www.csiet.org
The CSIET offers ratings on youth exchange programs. Visit the site for a listing of reputable programs that offer opportunities to get involved in environmental projects abroad.

International Volunteer
www.volunteerinternational.org
This organization offers volunteer opportunities of all kinds. You can search the Web site by region, country, type of work, and duration. It's also a resource for preliminary requirements for volunteering abroad.

Cosmic Volunteers
www.cosmicvolunteers.org
Unique programs available from Cosmic Volunteers allow you to work on a sustainable farm in India, a wildlife center in Kenya, or another project in Africa, Asia, and Latin America.

DIFFERENCE MAKER

Future Problem Solving Program

Snuggled among birch trees and salt lakes on the Western Siberian Steppe of Russia is the small town of Shchuchye. It's a place full of natural beauty and amazing views, but that's not the full story. Only a few kilometers from Shchuchye sit 6,000 tons of aging chemical weapons—enough arms to erase Earth's entire population three times. To make matters worse, the abandoned weapons lie unprotected in crumbling wooden barns surrounded only by a broken-down barbed-wire fence.

Does this sound to you like a serious environmental hazard and security threat? That's exactly what four teens at a high school in Appleton, Wisconsin, realized as they researched chemical-weapons dumps around the world. The students wanted to do something to help, but it was a long way from Wisconsin to Siberia. That's when the students came up with a plan to make the Shchuchye weapons situation a project of the Future Problem Solving Program, an organization that involves young people in solving real-world problems.

With local fundraising and sponsorship, the Appleton team was able to visit Russia and meet with peers from Shchuchye #2 School. The two teams discussed the chemical-weapons problem, their fears about what might happen, and what could be done. Planning together, the students decided that the first priority should be the protection

Connect

Future Problem Solving Program (FPSP)
www.fpsp.org
The students of Appleton North High School and Shchuchye #2 High School partnered together in the Future Problem Solving Program. The projects this organization sponsors encourage students to develop creative solutions to real-world problems. To find out more about the program, visit the Web site.

of the people. Then they would work toward destruction of the weapons.

There was a lot of work to do, and it wasn't done overnight. The Russian teens developed an evacuation plan, collaborated with local officials to distribute emergency instructions, and worked to provide students with protective clothing. In the United States, students at Appleton High raised funds, including for the installment of two emergency sirens in Shchuchye. They set up conferences to raise awareness about the situation and designed a Web site where visitors could purchase protective gas masks for the Siberian youth.

While these actions helped to protect public health in the short-term, they wouldn't permanently end the danger to Shchuchye citizens or eliminate the potential for environmental disaster. Destroying the weapons was the only long-term solution. The U.S. government had offered money to help build a disarmament plant, but

many people in Shchuchye resisted, fearing a facility would only increase the possibility of catastrophe.

To address local fears, the Russian students shared research with community leaders and residents on how the plant would work and what might happen if it weren't built. They demonstrated that the benefits of the project outweighed the risks, and finally convinced residents that building the plant was the best option.

The students—eleven time zones apart—cheered and shared virtual hugs over the news. Three years of hard work on two continents paid off, and a disarmament plant is today being built.

Said one group member, "This project has been the most profound, life-altering experience of our lives. We are a team—Russians and Americans. We are lifelong friends."

Youth Representation

" *People are so accustomed to thinking of youth as the future that they are surprised to be challenged to think of us as the present.* "
—Camilo Soares, 15, Global Activist

What Are the Facts?

Young people have traditionally been underrepresented in many ways. Some teens feel they're not taken seriously by adults—that they don't have a true say in what happens to them. Adults usually determine school hours, curfews, and many other daily decisions out of necessity, but often without getting feedback from the ones who will be affected by them. In most situations, age restrictions also prohibit teens from voting or fully participating in the political process.

Today's teens, however, are standing up more than ever and demanding to represent themselves. From positions on boards of education or student councils to youth memberships in political parties, teens are taking roles to speak for themselves and playing a part in decisions that affect them. The global youth movement is itself an example of increased youth influence.

Why are teens so important in facing the challenges of today? For one thing, they have a unique perspective, different from that of any previous generation, and a fresh approach to solving problems. Many young people are also more open to trying new things—rather than not doing something for fear it won't work. This section has lots of ways you can represent yourself and your generation.

Keep It Local

Join your school board or student government. Many school boards in the United States now include high school students as representatives who serve the board in an advisory role. Like those involved in student government, these young people are often elected by peers. Student representatives can have an important role in an administration's decision-making process. Take advantage of these opportunities to make sure your and your peers' interests are being considered at school.

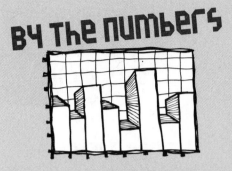

By The Numbers

Youth Representation:

➤ The voting age is currently 18 in most nations, though others (like Germany, Austria, and Brazil) allow 16- and 17-year-olds in certain cities and regions to vote. (The World Factbook, www.cia.gov/cia/publications/factbook)

➤ Hundreds of organizations around the globe are founded and operated by teens. (Global Youth Action Network, www.youthlink.org)

➤ Around the world, there are more teen politicians and entrepreneurs today than at any point in human history. (YouthNoise, www.youthnoise.com)

➤ Between 15 and 20 percent of school boards in the United States include student representatives, though most of these representatives serve in an advisory role. (National School Boards Association, www.nsba.org)

Camilo Soares

"We're going to have a student council," 15-year-old Camilo Soares said one day as he spoke with fellow students. Some of his peers weren't so sure. It was 1992, and not a single school in Paraguay had a student council. With some intense lobbying, however, Camilo and the others succeeded. Their high school in Machado, Asunción, became the first in Paraguay to form a student council. Looking back, however, this was really only the beginning of changes to come.

After the council had been formed, the students asked themselves, "Why not be in charge of the school?" The students knew as well as anyone what their school needed. And it seemed to them that they could have a greater positive impact if they had the final decision on some matters. With some strong powers of persuasion, the teens from Machado High School convinced the administration to turn over authority to students—not forever, but for 10 days of each academic year.

"During these days," Camilo explained, "students head all the departments. They can raise salaries and fire teachers, and their decisions have permanent effect, but they have to be able to justify them." The program was such a success that it was replicated all over Paraguay—50 schools enjoyed a week or two of student rule. "It is changing the concept of what a student is," said Camilo. "They are creators of the education system, not just spectators."

Practice forged true leadership—leadership that would be very much needed four years later. In April 1996, Paraguay's fragile democracy was threatened by a coup. It was the youth of Machado, under the leadership of Camilo, who stepped in. "Neither the church nor the political parties nor the traditional structures had any idea how to respond,"

Camilo said. "Everyone retreated to safety. Everyone, that is, except the nation's youth. We called them to the streets in defense of the right to live in an open and democratic society. We thought 20 to 30 people would turn out, but within a week there were demonstrations 24 hours a day, with 20,000 or 30,000 young people."

With the public obviously in overwhelming opposition to the coup, it collapsed and democracy was restored. Camilo knew, however, that his work was not done. He and his group started initiatives devoted to strengthening the democracy, increasing youth participation, and improving education programs. From student-council founder to national hero, Camilo continues his work to this day.

Become a juvenile justice advocate. You're probably aware that minors can be tried as adults for serious crimes in many countries around the world. This is a growing trend in some nations, with an increasing number of juveniles being tried in adult courts. Do you feel strongly about juvenile justice issues? Perhaps you'd like to take up the cause in one of the following ways.

- Involve yourself with school and community organizations that establish rules and punishments for teens. These groups sometimes create rules with no input from the people actually affected by the policies. You might take on issues like school suspension, curfews, or regulations for participating in extracurricular activities. You might also present information at organization meetings and work to influence opinions in other ways, including by covering issues in a student magazine or on a Web site.

- Explore opportunities for youth courts in your area. Youth courts give minors in the United States the opportunity to be tried and sentenced by peers. Many juveniles are first-time offenders who have committed petty violations. In youth courts, offenders are punished (often through community service and counseling requirements) but allowed the chance to amend behavior and clear their records of violations. Peers serve as jurors, attorneys, bailiffs, clerks, and even judges. You can find more information on the Federal Youth Court Program by visiting www.youthcourt.net.

- Advocate for just sentencing. In some cases, younger and younger juveniles are serving longer and longer sentences in adult jails and prisons around the world—even though studies show that juveniles are much more likely to be abused or assaulted in adult detention facilities. If this upsets you, consider forming a public campaign against the practice. You might also lobby public officials and demonstrate at court buildings.

QUICK TIPS

Getting Involved

When it comes to representing youth views, you don't have to stop at student government or the school board. Consider joining committees or councils working on an issue that's important to you—whether it's the humane treatment of animals, community beautification, or something else entirely. Look to get involved in any areas where you feel youth input is missing. What can you do if a group does not have youth positions available?

➤ Circulate a petition of peers' signatures requesting representation and voting privileges. An effective way to put pressure on a group can be to involve the media. Journalists are often excited to cover teen newsmakers pushing for youth representation. Make other adults in your community aware of your cause and seek their support.

➤ Become a youth advisor. Even if you cannot join a board or council as a voting member, you may be able to exert your influence by serving as a youth advisor. An advisory role can allow you to assert your views, ask questions, and make recommendations based on youth interests.

➤ Volunteer with a group. It's most often easier for insiders to gain representation on a council or committee. You might get your start with an organization by doing volunteer work. Positions of influence are more likely to open up for you if you've impressed and established the trust of a group.

Become familiar with your local government. National politics are covered in some depth on television, in papers, and on the Internet. Fewer people, however, are knowledgeable about local government. People ignorant of the political process are not in a position to advocate for themselves. If you could use some brushing up on how the system works, start by taking a tour of government offices near you. You might also go to a council meeting or a public address. Ask questions about how decisions are made and the role citizens have in debating them. Round out your knowledge by reading the charter of your city, hamlet, or district as well as any other important documents related to local governance. Once you have background on how the process works, you might get involved in some of the following ways.

- Become familiar with laws and ordinances under consideration. Propositions that can shape your community are continually coming before ministers, council members, and representatives—whether it's land use, mass transit initiatives, or other quality-of-life issues. Do your research on legislation and determine where you stand. Advocate for your position by petitioning, surveying, and interviewing the public.

- Serve as a volunteer within the government. Many times, local government is understaffed (and underfunded), which means there

may be intern or assistant positions available. Contact your local government to inquire about programs.

- Inform the public about community issues. It's great to learn about what's going on in local government, but it's even better to share what you know. You might maintain a Web site with city meeting minutes, legislative updates, and alerts on pressing neighborhood concerns.

- Speak on an issue in committee. Laws are often discussed in committees before coming up for vote. This is usually a stage at which the public can testify about the effects an initiative might have on their lives. Contact local officials to learn how you can get on the agenda to speak at these meetings.

DIFFERENCE MAKER

Ben Smilowitz

Ben Smilowitz started early in politics. In middle school, he campaigned in his home state of Connecticut with one of his state senators, who was running on an education platform. Ben was a strong advocate for young people being out on the campaign trail. He brought attention to youth issues that the senator also came to embrace during his time in office.

These two ideas—representation and education—have proven to be ones Ben can really support. At 15, he and a couple of friends cofounded the International Student Activism Alliance (ISAA), a youth-run organization working to expand the rights and representation of teens. First formed in 1996, ISAA grew quickly—chapters sprang up around the United States, some working to preserve first-amendment rights, repeal curfews, and tackle other teen issues.

One of the best things about the ISAA is that chapters are led by students at the local level—those who know best what their schools need. For Ben, it has never been about being in charge of a bunch of people. In fact, inspiring others to act is what really gets him excited. "I love speaking to my peers about getting active and working for change," Ben says. "I want to see participation rates in our society soar, and the only way to do that is to motivate students to get involved. I believe that peer-to-peer motivation is much more efficient than any other type of mentoring."

Ben never places limits on his expectations, especially when it comes to the things he cares about most. It's no huge surprise, then, that he helped author a bill debated in the Connecticut legislature—one that called for two student seats to be added to the state's board of education. In what was a large step forward for students, the law passed and students gained a say in their education. After the success of the Connecticut bill, others were introduced into state governments all around the country.

Ben knows how to draw a crowd and work to get things done. Given his motivation, you might want to keep your eye out for his name on a ballot near you someday.

Take It Global

Make your voice heard—represent! Join online forums to debate issues you are passionate about. News sites and blogs are great places to read what others are saying about a topic. You might join in the discussion with counter arguments and alternative solutions. The Internet is also a great place to gather large-scale support for your views. Post a message on a video-sharing site to outline your opinions and discuss how young people are affected by current events. Let others—including those at school, friends, and family—know about your online efforts, and encourage them to join your virtual community.

Plan an event celebrating International Youth Day. Celebrated on August 12, International Youth Day gives young people around the world an occasion to make their voices heard. Created by the United Nations in 1999, the youth holiday is also intended to make world leaders focus on issues affecting young people around the globe.

Connect

Voices of Youth
www.unicef.org/voy
UNICEF's Voices of Youth site offers information on pressing concerns in the world—from hunger and homelessness to youth rights. There are polls and discussion boards where young people comment on today's issues.

YouthNoise
www.youthnoise.org
Sometimes it takes a little noise to get things done, and YouthNoise provides the venue. Passionate youth users of the site discuss global developments on environmental issues, poverty and debt relief, world conflicts, and much more.

International Youth Day
www.un.org/youth
In many areas, debates and workshops on youth issues are scheduled for International Youth Day. These opportunities are often set up by governments and adult organizations, but you can also use the holiday as a platform to launch *your own* campaign on an issue you care about. Log on to the Youth at the United Nations Web site for some ideas.

DIFFERENCE MAKER

Ha Thi Lan Anh

On Tuesday and Thursday mornings in Vietnam, about 30 million young people tune their radios to "Voice of Vietnam." This isn't some fluffy top-40 pop music countdown, it's a hard-hitting news program on Vietnam's premier radio station. Written and produced by teens, it offers a fresh, youth-centric perspective on the topics of the day.

"Voice of Vietnam" was the idea of Ha Thi Lan Anh, who became frustrated when she realized that youth views weren't really represented in newspapers or on television or radio. As Lan Anh put it, "Adults could not actually know the thoughts of young people." So in 1998, 13-year-old Lan Anh decided to put her thoughts out there. She began to write and record stories on local issues. Some of her friends joined her, and together they formed the Young Journalists Group. Soon members of the group were placing articles in newspapers and spots on the radio. These reports were different from the other stories appearing in the Vietnamese media. They spotlighted the experiences and thoughts of young people around the country.

Rather than take the same old approach to the news, the Young Journalists Group challenged readers and listeners to consider fresh perspectives. Their stories inspired people to take action on important environmental, education, and gender-equality initiatives. A monthly newsletter and student magazine expanded the group's reach. And it wasn't only youth who were paying attention. Lan Anh convinced government ministers, congress members, and state social workers to discuss public policies in a series of TV and radio programs that she produced. Impressed by Lan Ahn, government officials invited her and other young journalists to give their advice on the National Action Plan for Children, legislation that outlined government youth initiatives through 2010.

Today, Lan Anh and her friends are as active as ever. "Voice of Vietnam" remains a radio sensation. The Young Journalists Group has produced over 500 radio programs and contributed hundreds of articles to more than 20 of the nation's magazines and newspapers. And after receiving recognition and awards from many international organizations, Lan Anh is sure to inspire other youth activists far beyond Vietnam.

Help to get out the vote.
Depending on your age and where you live, you may or may not be able to vote in local, regional, or national elections. Even if it will be a little while before you can cast an official ballot, you can still participate at the polls. How can you get involved on election day?

- Encourage your family, friends, and neighbors to vote. Many people feel apathetic about voting, thinking their vote will not make a difference. Join or form a campaign to get people reactivated in the political process. Remember—no vote is no voice.

- Help people vote. One of the reasons that voter turnout is low in many countries is that some people are unable to reach polling places on their own. This is particularly true of people who are handicapped, elderly, or without transportation. You might volunteer as a driver or companion, or participate in an absentee ballot initiative. Another group of people who vote in smaller numbers is nonnative speakers, who may find it difficult to get information on candidates in

Kids Voting USA
www.kidsvotingusa.org
This organization makes it possible for young people in the United States to visit official polling sites on election day and cast their own ballots on the same issues and candidates that eligible voters are deciding on. Look into how you can join or start a program in your community.

League of Women Voters
www.lwv.org
The League of Women Voters is an advocacy group working to ensure that all who want to vote are able to. Each election cycle, millions of people are disenfranchised because they don't have the means or information to cast a ballot. Log on to the site of this organization to learn how you can address problems in your area.

their own language. You might get involved by offering your services as a translator or by distributing campaign information in foreign languages.

- Work to increase youth participation in elections. Even if they cannot vote, minors involved in election activities are more likely to become committed voters when eligible. You might work on an existing campaign to turn out the youth vote, or set up a mock election online or at your school. Make the results of your youth vote available to those who participated.

Connect

National Youth Rights Association
www.youthrights.org
The National Youth Rights Association is a youth-led group working to lower the voting age in the United States. The organization believes it is unfair that teens are taxed (through employment) but not allowed a voice in selecting who will represent them. You can log on to the Web site to learn more about taking part in initiatives to increase youth representation and other campaigns.

Learn about efforts to lower the voting age. Did you know that proposals to lower voting ages have been made in many areas—including in countries such as England, Canada, Austria, and the United States? If you agree with these efforts, consider joining a campaign to expand youth voting privileges in elections.

Milos Jovana Savin

Milos Jovana Savin, 17, huddled in a darkened cellar with his friends in the former Yugoslavia. "How do we help our country?" they asked themselves. It was 1997, and Slobodan Milosevic's reign of tyranny had not yet ended. Among the people there was talk that there had been mass killings and torture—and fear over whether they might be next. Whom would Milosevic target? What would happen to the country?

Milos and his friends were afraid, but they knew they had to act. They formed their own youth organization, the Creative Youth of Novi Sad, and selected Milos as president. Meeting frequently, the group planned and marched in public demonstrations to protest the regime. Taking part in these activities demanded courage. The government, feeling threatened by the group, labeled Milos and the other members "foreign mercenaries" and "fascists." Given Milosevic's history of persecuting political

opponents, it seemed possible that group members might be arrested, perhaps even executed, for their actions. The Creative Youth of Novi Sad had to be careful to stay out of the target range of violent regime leaders.

During this period of the late-1990s, others in Yugoslavia were also beginning to reject Milosevic's rule. In 2000, national elections were scheduled. This might seem like it was a perfect solution to end Milosevic's tyranny—just vote him out! But things weren't that simple. People continued to live in fear—of what might happen under a new president, of retribution if not enough people voted and the government remained in power. It appeared doubt and fear would keep people from turning out to the polls and doom Yugoslavia to more years under the oppressive Milosevic.

It was at this moment that the Creative Youth of Novi Sad made a move to get out the vote. Milos and the other group members hit the streets, passing out thousands of leaflets, shirts, pens, and penlights (to be used in night vigils) with the message "Voting is the only way to build democracy." People took notice and gained courage. Momentum built and masses of people turned out to support the vote. On election day Slobodan Milosevic was soundly defeated.

The Creative Youth of Novi Sad had helped turn the page on a bloody epoch of Yugoslavia's history and on to a new, more hopeful one—one in which the country would be split up to diminish ethnic conflicts, one in which Milosevic would be held responsible for his crimes of killing and torture.

The Creative Youth of Novi Sad have since grown into a much larger organization. After the breakup of the former Yugoslavia, many needs emerged in the city of Novi Sad. Milos's group, along with U.N. organizations, is promoting public safety, health, and education programs. While some hard times remain ahead, the Creative Youth of Novi Sad seems certain to persevere. And its members will never be forgotten for giving people courage at a time when their country most needed it.

Advocate for youth issues around the world. There have been many strides for greater youth representation, often on the part of groups working at the international level. Some of these global organizations allow for the opportunity to travel around the world to attend meetings where youth issues are discussed. If you're passionate about youth representation, consider joining this global debate.

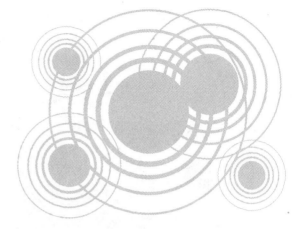

Youth Delegates to the United Nations
www.un.org/youth
This program through the U.N. allows teens to join a country's official delegation to the United Nations General Assembly. On the site you'll also find opportunities to lobby member states without youth representatives to allow young people to serve as delegates on their councils.

European Youth Forum
www.youthforum.org
Europe has been changing rapidly since the formation of the European Union, and policies and participation among member countries continue to shift. Made up of more than 90 National Youth Councils and International Non-Governmental Youth Organizations, the European Youth Forum serves as a bloc of support for fair youth representation in the union.

Model U.N.
www.cyberschoolbus.un.org
Model U.N. is a school-based organization that allows the world's young people to represent their views while also working toward initiatives of the Millennium Development Goals. Visit the Web site for information on how your school can participate, and get information on the United Nations and the most pressing issues of today.

Peace and Friendship

Peace won't happen just by talking.
We must change our hearts.
—Juan Uribe, 17, Global Activist

What Are the Facts?

There are currently about 30 armed conflicts going on around the world. Wars, most often, used to take place on battlefields, but today many conflicts occur where people live—on their streets and in their homes. Hundreds of thousands of people die each year in wars. When the rule of law dissolves, people often commit horrible crimes, such as torture, human trafficking, and sexual abuse. Armed conflicts can lead to displacement of whole populations, and countries bordering a battleground must absorb refugees. Even after violence subsides, war has deep and long-lasting social, political, and economic effects that can leave a country or region and its people devastated for years.

The causes underlying armed conflicts are often complex. Some people feel they have no choice but to fight for certain rights or causes. Most often, people have differing perspectives on whether violence is justified. Regardless of your personal convictions about armed conflicts, you can work to make the world a more peaceful and accepting place. It's all a matter of finding the cause and action that's right for you. This section offers many ideas for peaceful actions to help you get started.

Keep It Local

Promote peace and tolerance in your school or community. When people hear the word peace, they often associate it with war and bombs and guns. But speaking out against armed conflict is not the only way to promote peace and friendship. Here are a few opportunities to help create greater social harmony.

- Hold a "Mix It Up" event. Most teens hang out with pretty much the same people each day. A "Mix It Up" event can help you step outside of your comfort zone to meet and befriend new people. Venturing beyond your current group of friends allows you to meet people with interesting experiences different from your own. And learning about the lives of others can help create a closer, friendlier, more

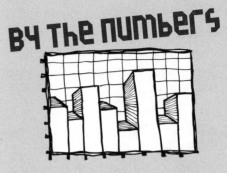

BY The numbers

Armed Conflicts:

➤ In over 30 countries, armed conflict is a daily reality. (Amnesty International, www.amnesty.org.)

➤ Because of conflict and oppression, 33 million people worldwide are displaced from their homes. (Doctors Without Borders, www.doctorswithoutborders.org)

➤ Over two million children have died as a result of armed conflict in the last decade. Six million children received permanent disabilities or serious injuries. (UNICEF, www.unicef.org)

➤ Landmines cause up to 20,000 deaths per year. (United Nations, www.un.org)

➤ An estimated 300,000 child soldiers under the age of 18 are involved in armed conflicts. (UNICEF, www.unicef.org)

accepting community. Visit www.tolerance.org/mixitup for information you can use to stage an event in your school or community.

- Plan a multicultural celebration. Ask people to share information about their cultural, ethnic, and religious backgrounds. This could include demonstrations on food, games, beliefs, clothing, and languages, just to name a few. You might set up an exhibition featuring cultural artifacts, films, or musicians. Consider commemorating the event by creating a collaborative mural that can serve as an enduring landmark of the commitment to tolerance in your community or school. One online resource you can reference is the Web site of Youth for Peace (www.worldpeace.org/youth), an organization that promotes tolerance through art, concerts, and peace poles—handmade monuments displaying messages of nonviolence in multiple languages.

Connect

Tolerance.org
www.tolerance.org
This Web site features many actions and advice for teens, teachers, and parents working to end hatred and bigotry in schools and communities. Log on for information and tools you can use to respond to hate speech, celebrate multiculturalism and diversity, and promote acceptance for all.

Youth Against Racism in Europe
www.yre.org.uk
Youth Against Racism in Europe operates programs in 16 countries. The organization focuses on stemming racism and stopping hate crimes. Log on to the Web site for ideas you can use to promote tolerance and learn more about volunteer opportunities available with the group.

Life-Link Friendship Schools
www.life-link.org
Based in Sweden, this program involves schools from around the globe in peaceful actions. More than 500 schools in over 70 countries have participated. You can find suggestions for peaceful actions in a free handbook available for download at the Web site. This program also offers student exchanges for those interested in taking this action global.

- Promote tolerance and safety for all students—regardless of race, religion, ethnicity, cultural beliefs, gender expression, or sexual orientation. For example, many teens feel afraid to go to school because they are harassed or physically abused because of their sexuality or gender identity. Gay-straight alliances (GSAs) are groups working to end the hate and create safe school environments for all students. For more ideas to promote tolerance, visit the safe schools site of the National Education Association (www.nea.org/schoolsafety).

- Speak out against injustices you observe in your community. Advocate for equal rights for all people—including groups that may be marginalized. You could send a letter or email outlining your position to the editor of a newspaper, a television station, or a Web site. You might also distribute pamphlets, pass around a petition, or confront local leaders about the role they play in promoting equal treatment and opportunity.

Make known your views on world conflicts. Don't take for granted the right to make your voice heard. You can support global peace through local actions. How?

- One way to advocate for peace is to send out your own public message of tolerance and nonviolence. You might use posters, stickers, or T-shirts to make your statement. Find some sample designs to get you started at www.anotherposterforpeace.org—or come up with a message of your own.

- Celebrate the International Day of Peace. The United Nations General Assembly declared September 21 of each year to be International Day of Peace. The event is marked in many ways around the world. Visit www.internationaldayofpeace.org to learn how you can mark the occasion in your community.

- You might join a public demonstration. Information on public rallies is often posted in community centers, alternative weeklies, and magazines. You can also find a calendar that lists dates and sites at www.unitedforpeace.org. Page 17 has additional suggestions for participating in demonstrations.

DIFFERENCE MAKER

Not In Our Town

A lot changed for everyone living in the United States after the attacks on September 11, 2001, in New York City; Arlington County, Virginia; and Somerset County, Pennsylvania. People who had emigrated from the Middle East were no exception. In fact, many Arab-Americans became targets of violence and intimidation. Some even grew afraid to leave their homes.

A group of Chicago, Illinois, teens witnessed these acts of intolerance against Middle Eastern students in their community. They were outraged that some people's response to terror attacks was to create more terror—in their own neighborhoods and toward their fellow citizens. When these teens heard that a hate demonstration had been held near a local high school, they decided enough was enough.

Channeling their indignation and compassion, these teens created five public service announcements (PSAs) to send messages of peace and unity to their community. The short videos contained strong, often unsettling footage, including real images of students taunting an Arab-American teen and images of the impact of war around the world. The Public Broadcasting Service (PBS) has picked up the effective and poignant PSAs and features them on the anti-hate Web site, Not In Our Town, sending the teens' messages of unity to the world.

Connect

Not In Our Town
www.pbs.org/niot
Not In Our Town is a campaign that promotes community action against hate crimes. The Web site, supporting a documentary of the same name, offers many ideas on how you can get involved in the anti-hate movement in your area. It also features true stories of successful Not In Our Town events and efforts, including the story of the Chicago PSA effort.

Spend time with people who have experienced war. A good way to better understand war is to speak with people who have been through it. You might have conversations with relatives or neighbors who are war veterans. Refugees of conflict are part of nearly every family and community. Consider recording the stories of the people you speak with. Share what you learn with others to actively promote peace.

Connect

Ancestry.com
www.ancestry.com
Are there people in your own family who have experienced war? Every generation of people, in nearly every region of the world, has been affected by conflicts. This site allows you to search your family's name using a variety of special search functions. A database of information extends back hundreds of years. After doing some looking online, pursue your research further by speaking with relatives about your family's story.

Veterans Affairs Voluntary Service
www1.va.gov/volunteer
In the United States, you can connect with people who have served in wars by volunteering at a local Veterans Affairs (V.A.) hospital. The V.A. Web site lists hospital locations, volunteer needs, and student programs. You might bring these opportunities to the attention of a teacher and propose a class project on the effects of war.

Juan Uribe

What would you do if someone shot and killed your father? Juan Uribe had to face this question at the age of 13.

It was 1996 and Colombia was amidst a bloody civil war. Juan knew that others would continue to die until there was an end to the conflict—more fathers, more mothers, more siblings, more friends. He hated the war that was destroying his country—the fighting had lasted for decades. Was there really anything Juan could do to help stop it?

Enter the Children's Movement for Peace, a campaign against the war that was killing Colombia's men, women, and children. Juan devoted himself to the cause to honor his father and help deliver his country to a new era. Despite threats from those who wanted violence to reign, Juan helped mobilize other members of the movement to support the Children's Mandate for Peace and Rights—a declaration

voted on and approved by some 2.7 million Colombian young people throughout the country. The declaration called for an end to the violence and a right to "survival, peace, family, and freedom from abuse." For their effort, Juan and four other members of the Children's Movement for Peace were nominated for the Nobel Peace Prize.

Colombia continues to experience unrest to this day. Juan and the Children's Movement for Peace, however, have made an important difference in the history of Colombia. For the first time in many years, hope for peace, reform, and freedom exists within the people. A new generation of leaders from the Children's Movement for Peace is on the way, and as Juan says, "If you harvest a child of peace, you'll have an adult who will not be violent."

Take It Global

Write in support of peace. Send an essay, editorial, or letter to the editor of a newspaper or magazine in support of your position on an armed conflict. Blogs and online message boards are other great places to voice your opinion. What if you have trouble finding the right newspaper, magazine, or Web site for your opinion piece? Maybe you can publish it yourself. Think about forming your own publication in support of world peace.

YouthNoise
www.youthnoise.com

Learn how to "make noise" about the global issues that matter most to you, and discover how to make legislators listen. The helpful Change the Rules Toolkit at this Web site provides invaluable advice on how to write to Congress, how to start a petition, how to lobby, and how to stage a nonviolent protest.

DIFFERENCE MAKER

The Olive Branch

Never underestimate the power of words to bring people together. Despite ongoing conflicts in the Middle East, there is at least one publication that promotes a more peaceful future in the region. *The Olive Branch* collects the writing and artwork of young people from countries including Afghanistan, Israel, Palestine, Cyprus, Egypt, India, Pakistan, Jordan, Turkey, and the Balkans. While violence and distrust continue to add to long-standing tension among these countries, those involved with the magazine aspire toward a future where all cultures will unify to celebrate and share values of peace.

In a single issue of the magazine, Greek and Turkish teens from a divided Cyprus express mutual hopes for peace and reconciliation; a young Afghan photographer shares images of the people and landscapes of her country, expressing both love for the country and sadness at its political unrest; and a girl from Mumbai, India, shares a poem on the futility of war.

There is a great willingness among many young people to create peaceful coexistence and friendship in the Middle East, even while violent and bloody battles surround them. *The Olive Branch* gives these teens the opportunity to speak and serves as an offering of peace—a demonstration of the unity that can be achieved among those who were once enemies.

Connect

Seeds of Peace
www.seedsofpeace.org
The Olive Branch is a program of the Seeds of Peace, an organization that sponsors leadership programs and cultural exchanges for teens from countries in conflict. Visit the Web site to learn about opportunities for getting involved. To view the current issue online, visit www.seedsofpeace.org/OBCurrentIssue.

Fundraise for an organization promoting international peace. As you know, you don't have to necessarily leave your home or city to make a difference in other countries around the world. There are many organizations working to keep the peace in places all over the globe. If you're unable to travel abroad but want your action to have global reach, you might fundraise for peace. Fundraising suggestions are given on page 15.

Connect

Save the Children
www.savethechildren.org
This organization is one of the largest in the world devoted to the welfare of children—including those hurt, displaced, threatened, or otherwise affected by war and civil unrest. The Web site details how funds may be donated to the organization.

Landmine Action
www.landmineaction.org
Did you know that people in countries affected by war often continue to die after a conflict is over? Landmines used during wartime often remain exactly where they were placed, leaving local populations to literally navigate minefields. Thousands of people each year are injured or killed. Go online to the Landmine Action site to help.

Peace Brigades International
www.peacebrigades.org
This organization, headquartered in the United Kingdom, supplies volunteers and resources to countries where disputes kill or threaten life. The group advocates nonviolent de-escalation of armed conflicts and seeks political solutions to struggles. Information on donating to the group is provided online at the Web site.

DIFFERENCE MAKER

Annalise Blum and Katharine Kendrick

Annalise Blum and Katharine Kendrick, two high school students from California, had read about genocide in their history books. They never imagined, though, that such acts of hatred and cruelty could occur in the present day. In 2003, however, stories and images of the genocide in Darfur (a region in Sudan, Africa) splashed across news headlines. Hundreds of thousands of Sudanese citizens were being killed or forced from their homes. The two girls in California were shocked—history was repeating itself. They knew they had to take action.

Annalise and Katharine embarked on a joint effort of fundraising and education in their community. They spoke at school assemblies, brought in guest speakers, and screened documentaries on the violence in the Sudan. At the same time, they sold green ribbons to their fellow students, teachers, and community members to raise money to buy chickens—a sustainable source of food—for the Sudanese refugees. Through their efforts, Annalise and Katharine raised enough money to buy over 1,200 chicks.

Unfortunately, the conflict in Darfur continues to this day. The positive news is that many aid agencies are involved in the region with people—like Annalise and Katharine—helping refugee families on their road to recovery.

Connect

Save Darfur
www.savedarfur.org
Visit this Web site to learn how you can get involved in the humanitarian effort to help people in the Darfur region of Sudan. There are opportunities to make donations, sign on with a local chapter of the group, and raise awareness about the genocide.

UNICEF
www.unicef.org
The crisis in Darfur is a primary focus for UNICEF, the international agency that responds to humanitarian needs around the world. Visit the Web site to learn more about the situation and what you can do to help refugees of the conflict.

Participate in a cultural exchange. Visiting another country can be an effective way to gain perspective on conflicts while promoting understanding. If you're interested in travel, experiencing new cultures, and extending friendship beyond cultural and national boundaries, think about applying for a cultural exchange.

Connect

Peace Child International
www.peacechild.org
Peace Child International gives young people the opportunity to promote peace and sustainable living through leadership development and participation. Based in the United Kingdom, the organization operates in 120 countries. Log on to the Web site to learn about opportunities for traveling abroad or serving as an ambassador for the organization in your own community.

One World Youth Project
www.oneworldyouthproject.org
This organization is made up of a network of schools in over a dozen countries engaged in carrying out Millennium Development Goals (see page 24). Programs are open to both middle and high school students. The Web site includes information on global exchanges and things you can do to get involved at your school.

Center for Cultural Interchange
www.cci-exchange.com
Participate in the School-to-School Exchange Program with another nation to promote peace and understanding. For example, your school could host a group of Spanish students for three weeks. Each group consists of approximately 10 to 20 students. There is no fee to participate as the host school. You could also visit a school in another country (for a cost), or your family could host a visiting student.

Connect

United Network of Young Peacebuilders
www.unoy.org
Join a global network of youth volunteers campaigning for peace. Based in the Netherlands, this organization advocates for policy change by involving young people in lobbying leaders of countries around the world. Look them up for volunteer opportunities abroad as well as ways to promote peace at the grassroots level.

Legacy International Global Youth Village
www.legacyintl.org
The global youth village involves approximately 60 other young people from across the globe. You will participate in workshops on democracy and share 10 days of joint activities in an exchange that develops peace and understanding.

Lions Clubs International
www.lionsclubs.org
This organization arranges cultural exchanges and youth camps in over 190 countries. Exchanges are four to six weeks long and camps last for one or two weeks. Visit the Lions Clubs International Web site for a full menu of teen programs, including art contests and service projects that promote peace.

DIFFERENCE MAKER

Michelle Divon, Lana Ayoub, and Tara Ogaick

Michelle Divon, Lana Ayoub, and Tara Ogaick disagreed during a post-9/11 class discussion about the Israeli-Palestine conflict. Michelle, 17, is Jewish and from Israel. Lana, also 17, is a Christian from Jordan. And Tara, 16, is a Muslim from Iran and Saudi Arabia. Michelle, Lana, and Tara are each daughters of ambassadors to Canada.

As the girls continued to discuss their opinions after class at their Ottawa school, the conversation quickly escalated into an argument between Michelle and Tara. The two girls ignored one another after that. In fact, there was a lot of ignoring going on. Michelle and Lana also chose not to acknowledge one another. It made for some awkwardness around school.

After a period of cooling off, however, Michelle spoke with Tara about their argument. Then they started talking about other aspects of their lives—situations or parts of culture they'd both experienced in the Middle East. At some point their differences of opinion were overshadowed by other things: shared beliefs and experiences they had in common. It was then that they became friends and agreed to do what they could to end the hatred that existed between their cultures. Lana agreed to help, and the girls became a trio—representing three cultures, three religions, three friends. A presentation to their classmates on the conflict in the Middle East outlined all perspectives while driving home the fact that all involved suffered. None had peace. None had security.

It might seem unlikely that three young women from the Middle East found one another in a Canadian school and brokered a peace accord. Using their unlikely friendship forged out of adversity, the young women hope to become diplomats themselves and promote dialogue among their respective countries in the Middle East. As Lana put it, "With time we discovered that communication was the key to solving the tensions between us." Michelle, Lana, and Tara hope people from their homelands can do the same.

Our similarities are far greater than our differences. . . . Just like we cannot shake hands with a clenched fist, we cannot make peace without looking each other in the eye.
—Michelle Divon, 16, Global Activist

Index

This index contains the names of many people and groups that make a difference. If you can't remember a name, check under *"Difference makers"* for people and *"Youth organizations to contact"* and *"Web-based resources and groups"* for groups.

About the Author

A former public school teacher, Barbara A. Lewis has received many awards for excellence in writing, teaching, and leading youth in service projects and social action. She and her students have been honored for community contributions by President Clinton and featured in many national magazines and newspapers, in *The Congressional Record*, and on national television. Barbara's books include *The Kid's Guide to Service Projects*, *What Do You Stand For?*, *The Kid's Guide to Social Action*, and *Kids with Courage*. Barbara is a sought-after speaker on topics including character development, service, and social action.

Other Great Books from Free Spirit

The Kid's Guide to Social Action
How to Solve the Social Problems You Choose—and Turn Creative Thinking into Positive Action
by Barbara A. Lewis
This award-winning guide includes everything kids need to make a difference in the world, from true stories to fill-out forms and resources. For ages 10 & up.
$18.95; Softcover; 224 pp.; B&W photos & illust.; 8½" x 11"

The Kid's Guide to Service Projects
Over 500 Service Ideas for Young People Who Want to Make a Difference
by Barbara A. Lewis
Hundreds of ideas for service projects, from simple to large-scale community efforts. Endorsed by Youth Service America. For ages 10 & up.
$12.95; Softcover; 184 pp.; 6" x 9"

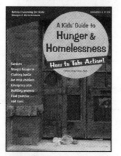

A Kids' Guide to Hunger & Homelessness
How to Take Action!
by Cathryn Berger Kaye, M.A.
Kids learn about the causes and effects of hunger and homelessness, read about what other people have done and are doing to help, explore what their community needs, and develop a service project. Includes write-on pages, resources, and a note to teachers and other adults. A hands-on, get-involved student workbook to use as a stand-alone or in conjunction with *The Complete Guide to Service Learning.* For grades 6 & up.
$6.95; Softcover; 48 pp.; 8½" x 11"

A Kids' Guide to Helping Others Read & Succeed
How to Take Action!
by Cathryn Berger Kaye, M.A.
Kids learn about literacy—the ability to read, write, and comprehend. They explore ways to improve the literacy of others, read what others (including ... eople) have done and are doing to help, explore what their community ... nd develop a service project. Includes write-on pages, resources, and a ... eachers and other adults. A hands-on, get-involved student workbook ... s a stand-alone or in conjunction with *The Complete Guide to Service ... g.* For grades 6 & up.
... oftcover; 48 pp.; 8½" x 11"

... r to request a free catalog of Self-Help for Kids® and
... aterials, please write, call, email, or visit our Web site:

Free Spirit Publishing Inc.
... e North • Suite 200 • Minneapolis, MN 55401
toll-free 800.735.7323 • local 612.338.2068
fax 612.337.5050 • help4kids@freespirit.com • www.freespirit.com